KING ALFRED'S COLLEGE
WINCHESTER

Religion in the Eighties

Concilium 141 (1/1981): Sociology of Religion

NEO-CONSERVATISM: SOCIAL AND RELIGIOUS PHENOMENON

Edited by

Gregory Baum

English Language Editor
Marcus Lefébure

T. & T. CLARK LTD.
Edinburgh

THE SEABURY PRESS
New York

January 1981
T. & T. Clark Ltd., 36 George Street, Edinburgh EH2 2LQ
ISBN: 0 567 30021 8

The Seabury Press, 815 Second Avenue, New York, N.Y. 10017
ISBN: 0 8164 2308 3

Library of Congress Catalog Card No.: 80 54383

Printed in Scotland by William Blackwood & Sons Ltd., Edinburgh

Concilium: Monthly except July and August.
Subscriptions 1981: All countries (except U.S.A. and Canada) £27·00 postage and handling included; U.S.A. and Canada $64.00 postage and handling included. (Second class postage licence 541-530 at New York, N.Y.) Subscription distribution in U.S. by Expediters of the Printed Word Ltd., 527 Madison Avenue, Suite 1217, New York, N.Y. 10022.

CONTENTS

Editorial

IN NORTH AMERICA many social scientists and some religious thinkers who at one time advocated social change in society and Church, have recently become defenders of the existing order and opponents of left-wing trends. In the United States of America these leaders of public opinion like to call themselves 'neo-conservatives'. Their reasoning against social change is on the whole not drawn from the conservative intellectual tradition; it is based rather on a new set of arguments taken from the social sciences and pragmatic considerations. Two articles in this issue (Steinfels, Baum) examine the neo-conservative phenomenon in the United States.

Are there similar neo-conservative trends in other countries? This is the question raised in this issue of *Concilium*. There are of course conservative trends in political and theological thought, based on a long and distinguished tradition. Classical conservatism in European thought has been the object of extended studies. This issue of *Concilium* deals with a different phenomenon altogether. It asks whether people who at one time favoured critical approaches and social transformation in Church and society, have recently changed their mind and become defenders of the *status quo*. The characterisation of neo-conservatism is purely descriptive. No one knows at this time, even after reading these articles, whether the shift of attitude, the turn to caution, the readiness to defend the existing order, are based on a community of ideas. Does the neo-conservative phenomenon have a definable essence? It is the hunch of this editor, after reading the articles of this issue and discussing the topic with prospective authors, that in the industrialised countries of the West neo-conservatism has in fact a common soul, a common rationale. But more research is necessary to validate such an hypothesis. The present issue of *Concilium* wants to make a contribution to this debate.

The reader will notice that the articles are not written from the same perspective. This corresponds to the style of *Concilium*. The first article (Holland) offers a persuasive explanation of the neo-conservative movement in terms of changes in the economic infrastructure, while the second article (Lasch) produces a set of cultural arguments for 'a backlash' against liberal and radical ideas. The European situation is examined mainly from the religious and theological perspective. One article (Grace) shows that the stand of the churches behind a united Europe includes opposition to political and cultural trends of socialist inspiration. Another article (Nivat) discusses the cultural impact of Solzhenitsyn's work. The revelation of the horrors of the Soviet system provides a negative legitimation of the western system despite its injustices. One article (Hebblethwaite) argues that for Pope John Paul II the experience of the Polish Church has a certain universal meaning. One author (Rousseau) examines the decline of the progressive movement in the Church of France. Another article (Sölle) argues that the new interest in existentialism need not have a conservative political meaning. Since it is well known that Joseph Cardinal Ratzinger and Hans Urs von Balthasar have had a change of heart in regard to the influence they wish to exert in the Catholic Church, two authors (Fahey, Kay) deal with their theological evolution. Is the charismatic movement in the Church a source of neo-conservatism? This question is examined by René Laurentin. Finally two authors, one Latin American (Richard), the other North American (Fleet), examine whether it is possible to speak of neo-conservative trends in Church and society of Latin America.

The articles do not offer an exhaustive account of the neo-conservative phenomenon. They are preliminary studies. It is too early to come to definitive conclusions regarding the nature of neo-conservatism and its impact on the Church. To the present editor at least it appears that what is taking place in the West is a crisis of liberalism: what is being questioned is the attention to personal autonomy, the reliance on positive sciences, and the progressivist assumptions. To many thinking people these trends have revealed their ambiguity: they have undermined human solidarity, they have weakened society's grasp on values, they have underestimated the power of the enemy, i.e., of those who have the power to organise the world to suit their own advantage. But where do liberals turn when these doubts emerge in their minds? They either search for community, defend traditional values and oppose the enemy perceived as left wing political trends (the neo-conservative option); or they turn to the left, opt for solidarity and against individualism, defend the unity of science and commitment and oppose value-free rationality, and recognise the enemy in the giant international corporations that control resources and production for practically the whole world. The reader is invited to read the following articles and make up his or her own mind on the meaning of neo-conservatism for the Church of Jesus Christ.

GREGORY BAUM

Edward Joseph Holland

Economic Crisis in the North Atlantic Nations

THE NORTH ATLANTIC nations, along with the rest of the world, are entering a deep economic crisis. It is hardly necessary to document the negative impact of persistent inflation, high unemployment, protectionist moves, capital flight, possible shortages in energy and strategic resources, climbing interest rates, unstable currency relationships, new worker austerity, etc. But there are different interpretations of this economic crisis, with different projections of social strategy and even different underlying assumptions about the nature of God, creation, and human community.

In what follows, I will propose one interpretation of our present economic crisis, with a sketch of some implications.[1] At the end I will try to contrast it with two other basic and conflicting interpretations. These three interpretations could be described respectively as 'radical' (the perspective of this essay), 'progressive' (or 'liberal' in US parlance), and 'conservative' (or 'neo-conservative').

1. A RADICAL INTERPRETATION OF THE PRESENT ECONOMIC CRISIS

The radical perspective proposed in this essay needs to be approached both historically (or genetically) and structurally. It consists of a paradigm of three stages of industrial capitalism.[2] These stages can be described chronologically as early, middle, and late capitalism. They can also be described substantively as the *Laissez Faire*, Social Welfare, and National Security Stages. (An attached chart gives an overview.)

We are presently entering the *third stage of late or national security industrial capitalism*. This period marks the final crisis of a process which has been unfolding for approximately two centuries. The crisis opens on to an entirely different period of human history. But what form that new period takes depends in part on how we respond to the present crisis.[3]

To understand this new stage, however, it is necessary to review the structural experience of the prior two stages.

(a) The *Laissez Faire* Stage

Early industrial capitalism, taking shape in the nineteenth century (especially the

1

STAGES OF INDUSTRIAL CAPITALISM

	I LAISSEZ FAIRE (Nineteenth Century)	II SOCIAL WELFARE (1900-1968)	III NATIONAL SECURITY (1968-?)
CAPITAL:	Local Family Firm	National Corporation	Transnational Corporation
TECHNOLOGY:	Labour Intensive	Capital/Labour Balance	Capital Intensive
ECONOMY:	Exploitation	Prosperity	Marginalisation
POLITICS:	Minimal State	Regulatory State	Authoritarian State
CULTURE:	Freedom as Licence for Entrepreneurial Few	Freedom as Social Opportunity for Many	Freedom as Security: Conflicting Definitions

second half), was a ruthless period. Social critics of the left and right (the Catholic Church often part of the right) were outraged by its injustices. But the injustices were not rooted in bad leaders, but in the deep structures of the changing society, which few really understood. Of these deep structures, there are two basic ones—the structure of *capital* and of *technology*.

First, in this early period industrial capital was predominantly *local*, that is crystalised into *family firms*. These firms, because they were small and numerous, were highly competitive.

The competitive relation of these small firms was aggravated by the *laissez faire* State, especially in the British Isles and North America. In this model the State refused to regulate the economy for the common good on the assumption that an unbridled free market implicitly served that cause.

This competitive structure created a vicious style of management which was forced to seek cheap labour and exploit it with long hours and harsh working conditions, or else face bankruptcy because of competition. In this structural environment, noble entrepreneurs were punished, while ruthless ones were rewarded. The suffering of the working class in this period has been well documented, although it was offset by harsh peasant backgrounds, by the lure of the city for youth, and by the horizon of hope in economic growth.

The second deep structure, that of industrial technology, also worked to create harsh conditions for industrial workers. Technology at this period was *labour intensive*, that is proportionately it used more human labour than machine power—due to limited energy sources (water and coal) and rudimentary machines (wood and leather only slowly replaced by iron and steel). The technology was therefore, by today's standards, unproductive. With low productivity, there were few consumer goods and little purchasing power. Hence social conditions for workers remained austere.

The ground of social struggle in this period was *economic*—against the exploitation of labour. The strategic form of this struggle was to create mass labour movements, often together with socialist or labour parties. In the North Atlantic countries, however, this struggle led only to reforms of industrial capitalism. Even western communist parties, despite the rhetoric, never achieved more than reform. That reform is the subject of the second stage.

(b) The Social Welfare Stage

The new social welfare stage, or middle industrial capitalism, took shape in the first half of the twentieth century. Its political expression in the regulatory and social welfare State varied chronologically from place to place (with Bismarck in Germany making pioneering innovations in the late nineteenth century, while the United States had to wait till the 'New Deal' of the 1930s).

The new stage was shaped by reform lobbies like mass unions, mass parties, and by religious pressures for change. But reform was amenable to the new stage only because of deep structural changes in capital and technology.

First, industrial capital was becoming maturely *national*, that is moving towards financing, production, and marketing on a national scale. This growing size of the enterprise required that it reach beyond the constraining form of the family firm, and hence there emerged the large, national *corporation*.

Ironically the national corporation was more favourable to labour, at least structurally. As corporations approached monopoly or oligopoly status, they had less threat from competition. Hence they could concede (reluctantly) to many of labour's demands for higher wages, pensions, and better working conditions without being undercut in the open market. Further, the emergence of the national corporation facilitated the very rise of national labour unions, so that workers now had greater social power to express their demands. Finally, the national corporation eventually required a regulatory state, which modified *laissez faire* theory, and provided a structural pressure point for positive social interventions into the economy.

Second, industrial technology was moving toward a *capital/labour balance*, and hence higher productivity along with continued labour absorption. This was especially made possible by the use of petroleum as a new energy resource, just as the national scale was facilitated by growing networks of transportation (motor vehicles) and communication (radio and telephone). The net result was the benevolent society of the industrial centres which we know from our recent past.

Thus we saw, in the North Atlantic nations at least, a more prosperous and less exploitive society. There was, however, little initial consciousness of the deep exploitation which remained at the internal and external peripheries of the system, nor of the deep racism and sexism embedded within it.

In this period, the centralised national State was the key structure upon which reform pressures were brought to bear by maturing mass movements. The State was thus the basic mediator of positive social change. Even communist societies, which emerged during this time as alternatives, shared this assumption of the central role of the national State, but they pushed it to more dramatic reaches by bringing the entire economy into the State sphere ('nationalisation'). The ground of social struggle in this stage was therefore *political*, that is a contest over the control and scope of the centralised national State.

(c) National Security Capitalism

This third stage, which we are now entering, is quickly undermining the benevolent aspects of the prior period (at least for the centre areas). It is precipitating a removal of class conflict in the North Atlantic countries, as well as providing deeper insight into the struggles against racism, sexism, and colonialism.

Again shifts in the deep structures of capital and technology are behind this stage change. The name of the new period, however, comes from the new form of the State (as was the case with the *laissez faire* and social welfare stages). The new form of the State is increasingly organised around the function of national security.

The national security State need not be only the overtly repressive forms we know from right-wing Third World dictatorships. Rather, in this paradigm, it includes a broader tendency in which the centralised national State aggressively moves to restructure the nation to maximise its security in the new global economic environment, or world market system. Of course, security here becomes more than military, although the predominant economic issues of security are increasingly intertwined with internal and external political and military questions. Thus the national security State is a growing development in First, Second, and Third World countries. But let us now look at the new economic environment.

First, industrial capital is moving to an unprecedented geographic scale and a new complex organisational form—the *transnational conglomerate*, operating on a global scale and including the horizontal and vertical integration of many distinct industries. Second, technology is becoming increasingly *capital intensive*, that is employing more machines and computers, using more energy and resources, but absorbing less and less labour proportionately. Both these changes are forcing the creation of a new society, for better or worse.

Transnational capital has become possible because of the new technological networks of communications (satellites) and transportation (jet travel), which facilitates the organisation of an enterprise on a world scale.[4] Also, the de-skilling process, by which the most complex technological products (e.g., electronic calculators) are now produced by multiple repetitive operations performed by low-skill workers (often young uneducated Third World women), make available a vast global labour force at extremely low cost (e.g., US$1.40/day in parts of the Philippines). Finally, the now more aggressive capitalisation of agriculture ('agribusiness') is converting massive numbers of peasants daily into urban marginals available as a reserve labour pool at the cheapest rates.

The net result is that, while capital and technology are more centralised than ever, new conditions of competition are being created across the labour markets of the world. Nations, and within nations regions, are being structurally forced to compete with each other to attract transnational capital to invest in their territory.

To attract investment, nations and regions are forced to offer 'attractive investment conditions', which include deeper exploitation of workers ('low labour costs'), curtailed social services for the poor and lower income sectors ('low taxes'), and soft or hard repression of unions and critical political constituencies ('stability and discipline'). These three conditions mean, more pointedly, aggravated class conflict, dismantling of the social welfare system, and erosion of democracy in favour of more corporativist or authoritarian government.

Internationally as the bi-polar stability of both the Cold War and détente yield to a more chaotic and volatile multi-polar world (generated by the maturing of transnational capital), external security issues become paramount. The nation must protect its competitive posture in the world market, and especially its access to strategic raw materials. This in turn puts strains on the Atlantic Alliance, destabilises East-West relations, and deepens the North-South conflict. As a result, the curtailment of social spending is paralleled by increased military spending, which in turn aggravates inflation and steals resources from the basic needs of the poor of the world.

At the same time, the situation is aggravated by the second deep structure, technology, now moving in a capital intensive direction. Since productivity is measured in terms of the capital productivity of labour (rather than of the social productivity of capital), the competitive situation pressures more rapid substitution of labour by technology. We are only now on the threshold of a whole new age of industrial robots and cybernated production. As a result, in this period capital can be said to cease absorbing labour and instead be displacing it. Thus along with the deeper exploitation of employed labour, there is the even more serious problem of *marginalisation* of unemployed or under employed labour. The North Atlantic nations, or at least many of them, are now marginalising their internal minorities by sending them home or confining them to internal ghettos where they become a permanent underclass. This tendency can be offset to some extent by negative population growth, but then people are being tailored to technology, and not the reverse. The problem of marginalisation is particularly acute for the young and the old. It is, of course, of crisis proportions in the Third World. The more rapid shift to technology also means more rapid depletion of natural resources, and in many cases increased pollution, so that the social crisis is interwoven with an ecological crisis.

These new structural changes are thus moving the North Atlantic community of nations into deep problems, of the same quality if not the same quantity as those formerly associated with the Third World. The benevolence of the social welfare period recedes, while the negative face of the *laissez faire* period reappears, but under different conditions and without the horizon of mere reform as was possible in the early period. Finally, the global social crisis becomes increasingly homogenous, in quality if not quantity.

2. THREE STRATEGIC RESPONSES TO THE CRISIS

There are basically three lines of strategic response to the crisis—the progressive (or 'liberal' in the USA), the conservative, and the radical.

The *progressive* strategy is simply a projection of the social welfare assumptions into the new conditions. This progressive response can be either reform capitalist (North America), social democratic (Europe), or even militantly communist. Basically it continues to focus on the centralised national State as the key mediating agency, either moderately by regulating the market with social welfare reforms, or militantly by nationalising parts or all of the economy into the State sphere. This strategy is quickly proving naïve, since in the new period it is transitional forces, not national ones, which are the primary shapers of the national experience. Further, the whole modern process, under both the liberal and communist ideologies, is continually undermining community as capital and technology are ever more centralised into massive bureaucracies—either public (the State) or private (the conglomerates as legal corporations). The progressive strategy therefore, by continuing to focus on the national State, misses the more basic issues on its transnational and local community flanks. For these reasons, the strategy is itself entering into crisis in the contemporary West. It looks to the future, but does not understand that the future is more than a projection of the centralised, national, social welfare State.

The *conservative* strategy (or neo-conservative in our discussion here) looks instead to the past. It sees the social welfare State as overburdened, and seeks to curtail it. It does this by mounting an attack on bureaucracy, on reformers, and on the 'new class'. Rightfully it looks back to local community and to mediating institutions as antidotes to the centralised, national State. The perspective, however, is ultimately a smoke-screen for the very forces which are daily undermining community and massing repressive power in an authoritarian or corporativist State. It does this simply by not addressing the deep structures which are at the root of the crisis, namely transnational capital and capital-intensive technology accountable only to private or State centres. These it entrusts to the 'free market' in a *laissez faire* framework which no longer exists. As a critique from the side of local community of the naïvete of progressives, the neo-conservative position has some lessons to teach. But as a critique capable of creating a more just and humane society, the neo-conservative position is a disaster. It reinforces the most dangerous right-wing forces emerging out of the crisis, precisely by allying itself with corporate power.

The *radical strategy* grows out of the socialist tradition, but also challenges some elements of it. It retrieves insights from the conservative heritage, like the stress on community and tradition, but ties them to a critique of the deep structures of capital and technology. Its basic principle is that *capital and technology need to be rendered accountable to multiple levels of human community, from the local to the global, through explicit mechanisms of participatory planning*. This principle differs from the conservative one by moving beyond nostalgia for community to focus on the deep structures which actually undermine it. It differs from the progressive one by criticising the key idea that the centralised national State is the only mediating agency for the control of capital and technology, and by insisting that control be mediated through multiple levels of community, from the local to the global. It also differs from the classical communist principle by arguing that the broad interests of community are ultimately repressed by a one-party vanguard controlling the centralised national State. Finally, it differs from all progressive wisdom by insisting that control over technology is not simply a matter of political control, but also of the cultural values embedded in a given technological path.

In conclusion, the ground of social struggle in this new period is precisely *cultural*. It is cultural in a two-fold sense: first, the basic task is now to build (or rebuild) multiple levels of human community, which is more than a political or economic task; and second, the struggle to build community is simultaneously a struggle over symbols and values. In the future, therefore, creative political organising and creative economic restructuring will follow, not precede, creative cultural vision.

The religious community, of course, has a profound role to play in this cultural struggle. The linkage of capital and technology with community and values brings religion to the core of the question and moves us beyond the Enlightenment assumption of the marginal or reactionary role of religion. The creative future, I suspect, is with some new synthesis of the religious and socialist spirits. In turn, the dividing line within religion, separating radicals from conservatives, will be the question of Utopian imagination.

Notes

1. This essay summarises the first chapter of a forthcoming longer study by the author on shifts in Catholic social strategy in the context of industrial capitalism, and on the meaning of these shifts for theology.

2. While the focus is on industrial capitalism (the model of the West), it is also possible to describe profound crises in the communist experience. Indeed one could speak of certain negative convergencies between industrial capitalist and industrial communist societies within the maturing world market system.

3. I take the economic crisis as foundational, but not determinative. On the contrary, there are several alternative strategic paths flowing from the economic crisis.

4. There are both private and public forms of the transnational enterprise. Thus both capitalist and communist industrial countries participate in this model, although the private form ('multinational corporations') presently predominates.

Christopher Lasch

The Conservative 'Backlash' and the Cultural Civil War

THE EVENTS of the Sixties and Seventies have opened a chasm, in American society, between 'opinion-makers' and 'middle America', between the culture of the professional and managerial élite and the culture of the masses. In the early Sixties, the new left set out to unite the forces of change around a programme of 'participatory democracy'. Breaking with the dogmas of the old left, the new left adopted a populist rather than a proletarian strategy of political action. Instead of appealing exclusively to workers, it tried to build a broad coalition of groups effectively dispossessed by the growth of irresponsible bureaucratic organisations like the corporation, the multiversity, and the Pentagon. It insisted that southern blacks, middle-class students, middle-class mothers, and other disfranchised groups had a common stake in opposing war, racism, and bureaucratic regimentation. Although the new left condemned many features of modern capitalism, it did not identify capitalism as the only source or even the principal source of oppression, and it condemned Soviet 'socialism' with equal vigour. The new left was not so much anti-capitalist as anti-bureaucratic. It saw large-scale organisation as the overriding fact of modern life and participation as the central political issue.

The ideas of the early new left were only half-formed, often superficial and naïve. Nevertheless they contained much political promise. With the advantage of hindsight, we can see that the new left was on the right track in intuitively gravitating to a Weberian rather than to a more strictly Marxian analysis of modern society. At some point in the middle Sixties, however, the new left took a series of wrong turns, which isolated the left from its potential constituency and generated, not a broad movement for social change, but a 'cultural civil war'. Instead of a coalition of the disfranchised against the organisation, the new left produced angry confrontations between revolutionary students and the police, largely recruited from the white working class. By 1972, the 'pigs' helped to elect Nixon president, and in 1972 they voted overwhelmingly to keep him in office. So much for the hope of a student-worker coalition.

There is no simple explanation of the collapse of the new left, but many of its failures can be traced in one way or another to its inability to achieve any kind of imaginative identification with American working-class culture. The turn to Marxism, in the late Sixties, did not help. Converts to Marxism talked a great deal about 'going to the workers', but when the workers instead of mounting the barricades demanded more law and order, leftists concluded that American workers suffered from 'false conscious-ness'. Even otherwise level-headed observers saw the 'cultural civil war' purely as a political backlash against the civil rights movement, the student movement, and the women's movement. In his often astute book on the student uprising, *The Radical Probe*, Michael Miles wrote that the 'student revolt has generated counter-revolt and a cultural civil war within American society. This "cultural civil war" . . . fundamentally, . . . is a simple political reaction, whose point is to suppress a radical movement which by its nature poses a threat to the *status quo* distribution of power and wealth.'

But why should 'middle Americans'—a category that includes workers, small tradesmen, and white-collar people—have such a heavy investment in the political and economic *status quo*? They have little wealth and less power. I think the 'backlash' has to be attributed not to their adherence to the *status quo* but rather to the failure of the left to address middle America with anything but contempt. The left values change, 'innovation', and the exploration of self, which it confuses with personal liberation. Middle Americans value continuity, stability, and personal responsibility. The left dismisses these values as reactionary and then wonders why it has no following among ordinary people. The enlightened, educated, 'progressive' classes look for an explanation of the cultural 'backlash' everywhere except to the failure of their own moral perceptions.

POPULAR RELIGION

Take the case of religion. The recent growth of 'non-traditonal religions'—of cults adhering to fundamentalist interpretations of religious truth and going in for faith-healing, snake-handling, shouting, and other forms of frenzy has occasioned much alarm in liberal circles. As we should expect, enlightened opinion scorns such bizarre expressions of religiosity as further proof of the backwardness of the proletarian mind. The struggle against religious fundamentalism, after all, has been one of the formative experiences of American progressivism. Ever since the Twenties, liberals have associated fundamentalism with rural reaction and have done their best to stamp it out. The discovery that they have failed, and that fundamentalism, far from being confined to benighted rural parts of the country, is spreading to the cities (and even making inroads among middle-class youth) comes as a rude surprise.

But surely the explanation of this development lies not in popular ignorance and superstition but in the failure of the mainline churches, Protestant and Catholic alike, which have capitulated so completely to the spirit of secularism that people turn to fundamentalism by default, as the only spiritual alternative to the industrial, bureaucratic, capitalist order. I do not mean that popular religions are explicitly hostile to capitalism or that they aim at its destruction. Most of them are completely apolitical. But they do speak to needs that capitalist societies have ignored. They are expressions, sometimes highly perverted and reactionary expressions, of the need for community, stability, and authoritative moral leadership; the need to find meaning and order in life; the need to submit oneself to a rigorous and demanding spiritual discipline, and to give oneself to a cause higher than the self. A culture of hedonistic self-indulgence cannot provide moral satisfactions of this kind, and neither can religious organisations that equate piety with psychic health and self-awareness.

The failure of the mainline churches does not necessarily lie in their political conservatism. The point is not that they are slavishly subservient to the political *status quo* but that they oppose to it a bankrupt vision of social change, one that culminates in a cult of politics and the State, and confuses political change with spiritual salvation. Reinhold Niebuhr's critique of the social gospel remains compelling today, and it has implications that reach beyond the failure of religious institutions to the general failure of the American intelligentsia. The social gospel, in the beginning at least, represented an attempt to recover some of the original meaning of Christianity and to identify religion with the interests of the common people. But the preachers of the social gospel, according to Niebuhr, in their effort to make the Church socially relevant ended by absorbing the secularised culture of progressivism and giving it a religious veneer. They not only became social reformers, socialists, and even revolutionaries—which was perhaps a step in the right direction—they began to identify socialism itself with the kingdom of God. Some of them even became apologists for Stalinism on the grounds that communism represented the highest form of moral perfection. The exponents of the social gospel, according to Niebuhr, forgot that the aim of political action is not moral perfection or brotherly love or any other kind of salvation but justice. As two followers of Niebuhr (Will D. Campbell and James Y. Holloway) have recently put it, the social gospel preachers went out into the world (which was no doubt better than political retreat) but took little of the Church with them. 'We have turned to the more scientific and neutral documentation for such preaching as we have done on the subject [of social justice and racism. Having rejected fundamentalism,] we turned away from seeking answers in the Scriptures. Our flocks have rejected social analysis and political meddling as none of the preachers' business—as they should have done (though their reasons were wrong)—so that our congregations have been left to flounder in the mire of religion. . . .'

FAILURE OF STANDARDS

I do not know of a better explanation of the collapse of the civil rights movement, at least in its cultural and religious dimension. The genius of Martin Luther King lay in his ability to politicise religion without giving up the idiom of unsophisticated popular religiosity. Most of his allies, however, most poignantly in the case of his white allies in the South, were uncomfortable with this idiom and sought to justify political action against racism with arguments drawn from modern sociology and from the scientific refutation of racial prejudice. In doing so, they ceased to offer their congregations anything specifically religious, anything that could not just as easily be found in institutions of higher learning or studies of the race problems sponsored by foundations or the reports of governmental agencies. Since their congregations were looking for religious guidance, not sociological expertise, they turned away from these 'pathetic efforts to inject morality and high-mindedness into politics'—'to bring moral dimensions to the great issues'—and embraced fringe churches that are fundamentalist, apolitical if not downright reactionary, and often militantly anti-intellectual as well.

Gary Wills makes a similar point about Catholicism, whose recent history, he argues, shows a 'basic failure in authoritative standards'. The presidency of John F. Kennedy, which coincided with the papacy of John XXIII, seems to herald a Catholic revival, just as the civil rights movement in the same period seemed to represent the cutting edge of social change. The hopes of the early Sixties—the ruins of which we live in today—seemed to be embodied in those heroes of the modern Church, King and Pope John, and also in Kennedy's New Frontier. But instead of stamping its imprint on the modern world, according to Wills, the Church capitulated to it. Catholic liberals took Harvey Cox's celebration of consumerism and the secular city as the last word on modernism. Cox in turn acknowledged the influence of Teilhard de Chardin, whose works enjoyed a posthumous vogue in the Sixties because they managed to equate spiritual progress with technological progress. Another admirer of Teilhard, Sister Jacqueline Grennan (later Mrs Wechsler), president of Webster College and then of

Hunter, spoke of him as the 'one who had the most profound influence on my own thinking'. Her eagerness to identify herself with the cause of progress, her efforts to 'laicise' Catholic education and to get rid of the 'medieval habits' worn by nuns, her boundless admiration for Kennedy and his New Frontier, her ceaseless travels to attend high-level meetings and to introduce the Catholic point of view into high-level discussions of world problems, in short her 'hopefulness toward any new situation', as Wills puts it, exemplified the Church's surrender to the dogma of progress. In view of all this, it is not surprising that a real Catholic radical like Daniel Berrigan moved away from his early infatuation with Teilhard to an understanding of our 'obscene Olympianism based on technology'—even as he moved toward a 'gospel conservatism', thereby retracing (in a different form and in a Catholic context) Niebuhr's spiritual and political journey, forty years earlier, from the social gospel to a new kind of political radicalism based on dogmatic religion.

'Much serious religion tends, today, to be politically radical and theologically conservative', according to Wills. The point can be stated in broader form: political radicalism increasingly has to identify itself with positions usually identified with cultural conservatism. Political conservatives have too long monopolised the values of family, law and order, patriotism, and continuity, and it is time for radicals (if indeed it is not already too late) to reclaim the ground that they have ceded to their political opponents. The problem is not merely one of political tactics. The culture of scientific enlightenment, therapeutic morality, and personal hedonism has developed by turning its back on the world of experience, which includes not only practical know-how but the collective traditions of humanity—'those divine reservoirs of collective experience, religion, science, art, philosophy, the self-subordinating service of which is almost the measure of human happiness', as Van Wyck Brooks once observed. The resulting gap between knowledge based on experience and knowledge based on scientific or pseudo-scientific analysis expresses itself politically in the ascendancy of the expert, the ascendancy of a professional and managerial class which monopolises esoteric information inaccessible to laymen. Culturally it takes the form of the so-called crisis of the humanities. The study of history, religion, and philosophy now either models itself on science or confines itself to 'values clarification', which in practice usually boils down to putting the best possible face on the actions taken by men of power. Because sophisticated knowledge has given up the task of refining and criticising experience, because it no longer addresses common problems or uses common speech, common people are turning to superstitions and 'floundering in the mire' of faith-healing and spiritual quackery.

However unattractive these manifestations of the spirit may strike sophisticated observers, the needs that produce them can no longer be ignored or stigmatised as culturally backward. On the contrary, it is in many ways the culture of modern scientific and humanistic enlightenment that is backward, and its failures are becoming more obvious, and more appalling and dangerous in their consequences, with the passage of time.

Georges Nivat

The Cultural Influence
of Solzhenitsyn

IT IS difficult to talk about the influence of Solzhenitsyn. He was instantly known to the entire world as a result of the publication, in issue No. 11 of *Novy Mir* in 1962, of his *A Day in the Life of Ivan Denisovich* (because this publication marked a definitive break with a taboo, that on the camps spawned by socialism). He then kept the world waiting with baited breath when his duel with the Soviet Government took a dramatic turn that reached its climax with his arrest on 13 February 1974, followed by his spectacular banishment. Opinion in the West was fascinated by the image of the rebel leaving behind him the famous 'Appeal from Moscow' (*One Word of Truth* . . .), addressed to the most monolithic power on earth. The appearances on western television which followed, and the vitality, the humour, even the joy of the born fighter which he evinced there, captivated immense television audiences. Not everybody has read the 2,000 pages of his chef d'oeuvre *The Gulag Archipelago*, but everybody is now acquainted with the words 'dissidence' and 'gulag'. These terms have become part of the universal vocabulary and are even sometimes used in a sense radically different from Solzhenitsyn's own. We do not need further proof of this fact than to recall, for example, that a special number of the French review *Tel Quel*, published in the summer of 1978, was devoted to the very notion of dissidence (and includes an article about the 'dissident' Pasolini, on the morrow of his murder). Again that the last chapter of the book by the sociologist Serge Moscovici, *Psychologie des minorités agissantes* (Paris 1979), deals with Solzhenitsyn as a 'minority' writer. Likewise the Catholic writer Corinne Marion has just published her *Qui a peur de Soljenitsyne?* and she there suggests that a return to traditional morality, say, in matters sexual, can in the context of the prevailing permissiveness of the day represent an act of authentic dissidence.

1. RECEPTION AND RESISTANCE

We really need an entire book on the way Solzhenitsyn has been 'received' in every western country (not to speak of Japan or India, where he is widely published). This is not only because we can see that every western country has its own specific way of responding to him, but because the way in which every western country has received and, specifically, resisted, Solzhenitsyn has evolved, has a history.

I use the term 'resistance' here advisedly because it is plain that Solzhenitsyn makes demands on our contemporary world, that these demands have had a great impact everywhere and that people have gradually begun to express their opposition. To take France, for example, there has been for a long time misunderstanding about a Solzhenitsyn who, on the one hand, had been appropriated by socialists (and he would in that case be a critic of socialism at once internal, naïve and 'plebeian', as Lukacs has written), but who, on the other hand, had then revealed himself to be a believer. The French Left quickly became divided about him. The communists today see in him an ideological adversary, whereas *Lettres Françaises*, Aragon's weekly liquidated by the party in 1972, made a notable contribution to his defence at the time he received the Nobel Prize. Pierre Daix has remained the only unconditional champion of Solzhenitsyn, but Pierre Daix is today on his own. Jean Daniel, in *L'Ere des ruptures*, has described very well the way in which recognition of Solzhenitsyn has been a stumbling block to the whole of the French Left, whereas in *Quel beau dimanche!* the ex-communist writer Jorge Semprun reviews his own experience of the Nazi camps in the light Solzhenitsyn has cast. On the other side, Max-Pol Fouchet has several times written and said publicly that Solzhenitsyn is a 'war-machine against the USSR, socialism, and the union of the left'. Solzhenitsyn's remarks in *The Gulag Archipelago* about general Vlassov, that brilliant Soviet general who agreed to collaborate with the Germans once he had been taken prisoner, have been maliciously distorted on the occasion of a memorable television programme, in order to insinuate that Solzhenitsyn was a traitor.

Religious people took some time to realise Solzhenitsyn's religious nature. This realisation came to expression the first time in *L'Esprit de Soljenitsyne*, the work of the Orthodox philosopher, Olivier Clément. The 'annexation' of Solzhenitsyn was here exaggerated; the whole warp and detail of the fictional fable was subjected to a symbolic exegesis which, in the final analysis, empties, or runs the risk of emptying, the real Solzhenitsyn of his principal quality: his lived energy. There has been no want of other religious commentators since: from a few very fine articles by Stanislas Fumet to the recent work of Corinne Marion. But there is no doubt that the most extraordinary homage has come from the so-called 'new philosophers': A. Gluckmann, Bernard-Henry Lévy along with the novelist Philippe Sollers, the former grand-master of French Maoism in the review *Tel Quel*, who struck the most resonant formula yet applied to Solzhenitsyn: the 'Dante of our time'.

We cannot sum up the way Solzhenitsyn has been received in every country, even briefly. Let us be content with indicating a universal phenomenon: an initial, unanimous welcome (as long as Solzhenitsyn's philosophical and religious premisses remain undisclosed) followed by the emergence of points of resistance. This is what happened in Spain, after Solzhenitsyn's declaration about the softening of Franco's dictatorship in its last days, in England after his resounding denunciation of the surrender to Stalin of millions of displaced persons of Soviet origin by Atlee's government, in the United States after the speech he delivered at Harvard in May 1978, denouncing America for its lack of will-power and even of virility. In each case, people were immediately up in arms. The editorial writer of the review *Nation* compared this speech with the one given in the same place, on the same theme, thirty years before, by the then Secretary of State, George Marshall. Marshall called upon the West to galvanise its energy under the banner and with the help of the 'supreme democracy of the world', whilst Solzhenitsyn, honorary citizen of the United States (in the line of Lafayette and Churchill) lashes a jaded and errant continent. The most vehement protest made at that time was that of the émigré Polish writer Jerzy Kozinski, a survivor of Hitler's holocaust: 'Whilst I share Solzhenitsyn's despair about the millions of people who died as a result of totalitarianism, I believe that he has not been able to understand that democracy is at best a shifting state swung between the tyranny which it has overthrown and the tyranny which it could become'. And it is just about the organic relationship that there is between democracy and religion that disagreement has most frequently arisen between Solzhenitsyn and his critics in the West.

I should like to conclude this all too brief summary by indicating the virulent polemic that is being conducted at present between different members of the Soviet emigration. This polemic originated in the already long-standing controversy which pitted Sakharov, the author of *Progress, Coexistence and Intellectual Freedom* (1968),[1] against Solzhenitsyn who replied in the opening article of *From under the Rubble* (1975), and this particular controversy is but a variant of the inexhaustible debate conducted against the backdrop of religion between Slavophiles and westerners within Russia itself. Solzhenitsyn is today often enough accused of narrow nationalism, theocratic ambitions. He has been called a Russian 'Khomeini'. The heirs of the 'democratic movement', Sinyavsky, Etkind, Amalrik, as well as Alexander Zinoviev, the author of *The Yawning Heights*, denounce the danger of his sort of thinking. They join a numerous and heterogeneous company which includes, for example, the American historian Pipes who has discerned in the Harvard speech hidden references to the works of the famous and ultra-reactionary procurator of the Holy Synod (and a friend of Dostoevsky) Pobedonostev, or the former French delegate to the Third International, Boris Souvarine, who wrote the famous book *Stalin* (1939). Souvarine accuses Solzhenitsyn (albeit with great respect) of caricaturing Lenin in his *Lenin in Zürich*, and of exploiting for his purpose the 'legend' of the German money and the 'sealed' carriage. The issue here is about the nature of Stalinism: Is it the logical sequel to Leninism or its betrayal (a thesis spectacularly defended in its time by Trotsky who illustrated it by drawing a parallel with the French revolution and 'Thermidor'). And I pass over a multitude of other misguided articles, riddled with references to Solzhenitsyn's 'doubtful' past. The Soviet machine has fabricated many works destined for foreign use over the signatures of old friends of Solzhenitsyn. Strangely enough these insinuations can be found once again in a Russian review published in Israel, *Vremya i Mui* (*The Times and Us*).

2. THE PRIMACY OF ETHICS

Solzhenitsyn's influence on our time is immense, even if, as we have just seen, there is a great deal of resistance to this influence. And in my opinion, what we have to start from is this capital fact: Solzhenitsyn has restored the primacy of ethics to the written communication, to literature. Here he is swimming completely against the current. Against all the champions of art for art's sake, against all the new rhetoricians of structuralism, against the 'new novel' and the death of character in literature, against the precious and the cynical, as well as against all the din of the prevailing schools and the media, he has solemnly re-established the Platonic triad of the true, the good and the beautiful. And as his ally in this he has taken the agnostic Albert Camus, whose Stockholm speech he quotes abundantly. Like Camus he proclaims that beauty makes free. Like Camus he declares that the artist has two aims: 'the refusal to lie and the resistance to oppression'. *The Gulag Archipelago* carries the sub-title 'An Experiment in Literary Investigation'. This is in the first place because art alone can transmit history where it has been systematically manipulated, so that the death of millions has been spirited away, the industrial production of a refuse of humanity in twentieth-century concentration camps, has been camouflaged (and we should bear in mind our own manuals in the West: the account is abstract, ideological, cuts out personal testimonies, restricts itself to resolutions of congresses). And the second reason is that it is

Solzhenitsyn's total conviction that only the work of art, combining as it does the beautiful and the true, is capable of unscaling men's eyes and conquering organised lying, even if it deals with what is most ugly in our time. *The Gulag Archipelago* is, therefore, not only an immense investigation (in which Solzhenitsyn has had the benefit of the voluntary assistance of hundreds of helpers), an encyclopaedia of existence in concentration camps, but also a work of art which draws us with the skill of a master into the 'catharsis' of Greek tragedy.

The cultural influence of Solzhenitsyn has a direct connection with three great 'No's' articulated by this writer-prophet. I should, therefore, like in the first place to sum up these three 'No's'.

It is doubtless one of the marks of the prophet or the reformer always to start with a 'No'. 'No' to ease, 'No' to debauchery, 'No' to the deviation of their people. Now we find a progress in Solzhenitsyn's thinking and in the literary creation articulated round these three successive 'No's'.

3. THE THREE 'NO'S'

(a) The Stoic 'No' to slavery of conformism

The first 'No' is the one the *zek* (the Soviet convict) utters to his condition and, for that matter, to every totalitarian ideology. A picturesque character in *The First Circle*, Professor Tchelnov, proudly answers the appropriate question in the questionnaire as follows: 'Nationality: *Zek*'. The *zek* is the slave of modern times, the inhabitant of the country 'where ninety-nine people cry and one laughs' (an expression which serves as the survivors' password). This 'No' on the *zek*'s part represents in the first place an 'uncurving' of the soul, a victory over the isolation that enrols one in the company, the rediscovery of community between the convicts; it releases the liberating laugh, the satirical reappraisal of history in the black light of the archipelago. The whole of Solzhenitsyn's work is marked by the dark and violent laugh of the *zek* for whom the cultural and historical heritage of past humanity has to be measured against the yardstick of the incommensurable constituted by the system of extermination by concentration camp. Jorge Semprun has hailed the flame of irony which sweeps *The Gulag Archipelago* and the birth of revolt along (in Book V of *The Gulag*, in the extraordinary chapter 'The Forty Days of Kengmuir'): Semprun draws our attention to the fact that Solzhenitsyn there rejects both classical humanism and Christian non-violence. 'But one has to have copped it for twenty-five years for nothing, put on an identification number four times, always kept one's hands behind one's back, been searched morning and night, extenuated by work, dragged to the BOUR (the disciplinary hole) in order to find that there, at the bottom of this pit, all the speeches of the great humanists seem to be like the chattering of well-fed Pekinese.'

This first 'No' of Solzhenitsyn is non-Christian, or, rather, pre-Christian; it is the 'No' of the Stoics based on human dignity. It is the dignity that is born from a refusal, which is expressed in the elimination of an informer. . . . The whole of *The First Circle*, an immense medieval dialogue as between knights of the grail, is a quest for honour and it is in virtue of a similar sense of honour that these new 'Rosicrucians' come to be detached from their slavery, become free in the very midst of their prison. This first stage of Solzhenitsyn is dominated by an idea of renunciation that is not so much Christian as Stoic. And what Ivan Denisovich exhibits is a sort of self-possession and dignity that is Stoic in character. His companion is the Christian (Baptist) Alyosha, but at this stage Alyosha is only tangential in Solzhenitsyn's vision. And who could say that the delight Kengmuir takes in his revolt ('Let's cut the informers' throats') is Christian?

This first 'No' of Solzhenitsyn is anchored in an indelible existential experience, that of the gulag and of the discovery of human autonomy in the depths of humiliation. Ideologically, Solzhenitsyn at this stage still relies upon the wise men of classical antiquity; not only Marcus Aurelius and Epicurus but also Lao Tsu. Now it is in this 'No' of Solzhenitsyn that all this century's survivors of the concentration camps have recognised each other: the Daix's, the Semprun's, the Wiesel's of our world. Solzhenitsyn has given artistic expression to the experience of life in a concentration camp; this is so difficult to think about that many survivors have not been able to speak about it for remaining closed within themselves after their liberation. Solzhenitsyn's first contribution here is universal and is not specifically Christian; he has given a form and offered a catharsis to the slave of the concentration camp, and he has restored the significance of human autonomy. He has thereby rejoined the greatest philosophers of classical slavery. He has imparted a certain painfully won meaning to the meaningless of totalitarianism, given it back a sapiential quality.

(b) The Christian 'No' to Greed

Solzhenitsyn's second 'No' is specifically Christian. He seems to have made the transition gradually. He does not appear to have had a sudden conversion but to have experienced a progressive 'transverberation' at the hand of God, punctuated by the discovery of the relative fragility of the Stoic wisdom he had refound and of the neglected figures of certain authentic saints (whether in the gulag or in the villages of Russia: Matronya's place). The 'Prayer' which I published in the Cahier de l'Herne in 1970 was one of Solzhenitsyn's first directly Christian statements. And even so his Christianity was still very discreet and operated as it were by reflection back. This is the theme of Cancer Ward ('the radiance of the Eternal'), it is the quick of Oak and the Calf (a dissident's tactical manual against the Goliath of bureacracy), and it consists in an intimate conviction of being armed by God, a faith in providence. In fact it is in this connection often tempting to speak of an Old Testament Christianity. The figure of Christ is absent, although his words do reverberate here and there ('Take up your bed and walk', Oleg hears in Cancer Ward).

This second 'No' is addressed above all to the rapacious, to the sated, the satisfied. When he was freed from the camp Solzhenitsyn was tempted by the intoxication of convalescence but, despite his evident passion for work well done and his taste for engineering, he refused permissiveness—whether of the cynical variety prevalent in Soviet society or of the liberal variety characteristic of the western economy, with its unbridled appetite and its ideology of uninterrupted progress and 'happiness'. All this was present in the apologia of a tale, Matronya's Farm. But the implications were not immediately seen in the West: an uncompromising condemnation of greed wherever it is to be found. The principal markers here are Letter to Soviet Leaders (1974), Message from Exile and the Harvard Speech (1978), Warning to the Western World (1980). Solzhenitsyn's appeal becomes twofold: self-limitation for all and, for the chosen few, self-sacrifice. The call to self-sacrifice is the measure of an individual's or a nation's spirituality. The survival of the world depends on the number of people who are willing to sacrifice themselves. 'The first handful of men to pass through the terrible filter will define themselves on their own, during or after the ordeal, when they identify with each other.' Honour was the first thing Solzhenitsyn's 'No' won, holiness is the second, and it is reserved for the 'elect'. A new 'chosen people' will form on the other side of the filter and its first characteristic will be neither their productive capacity nor their level of well-being but the 'purity of their mutual relationships'. Solzhenitsyn takes this ideal over from anarchists like Bakunin and Kroptkin (quoted in Cancer Ward) and he openly sets it in the light of Christ. It is the 'freedom from care' preached by Christ which governs his vision. For Solzhenitsyn this Christianity is at once ready for self-sacrifice, grounded in self-limitation and inclined to manage the earth frugally, and he finds it represented less by Orthodoxy (which he professes) than the Russian dissenters of the Old Faith symbolised by their protopope Avvakum and persecuted to the end of the nineteenth century by the official Church. Solzhenitsyn comes back to this time and time again. For him the Old Believers demonstrated the best of the faith. Contrariwise, we also find him condemning (rather rapidly) the Renaissance and the Reformation, the western (and above all Protestant) marriage of the ideas of election and progress. Solzhenitsyn's asceticism, his predilection for the eremitical life, the constant opposition to money-mindedness, his call to sacrifice, the attention he devotes to the gesture by which the warrior breaks through the barriers of biological egoism—all this has formed a second pole of fascination. He has brought back into our culture values that seemed archaic and he has resuscitated them brusquely by showing the West that it has been living out 'infantile' values.

(c) The Old Russian 'No' to Planetary Exploitation

His third 'No' is, I believe, a 'No' to europocentrism. This is perhaps where the Russian tradition of Slavophilia and Occidentophobia weighs most. But it would be petty to reduce this 'No' of Solzhenitsyn to the influence of Dostoevsky's *The Diary of a Writer* (which undoubtedly influenced him greatly), or of the Slavophile and Byzantinolatrous Leontiev (from whom he borrows many of his arguments against liberalism) and even less of Pobedonostev, as the American historian Pipes claims. Solzhenitsyn is an engineer and a mathematician, he is passionately concerned with the problem of managing the economy of this world's goods, he has read the Club of Rome's report, and he believes that the European and 'wordly' conception of happiness as a maximisation of an individual's or a nation's space is fundamentally mistaken, calamitous. He therefore advocates a frugal management of our planet, a voluntary self-limitation on the part of each individual, and a withdrawal on the part of the Russian nation to its own arid territory, far from the 'temptations' of the lands of the Mediterranean and the West. What this amounts to is that in his vision of a planetary 'fast' he assigns his own people an exemplary role, alongside that of other peoples similarly quickened by the yeast of the religious spirit (such as Israel or India). The standardisation of the earth, whether in its Marxist totalitarian form or in its rapacious capitalistic form strikes him as carrying the danger of something like asphyxiation. In any case Solzhenitsyn's nationalism cannot be suspected of expansionism since what it demands of Russia is a voluntary *withdrawal* and predicts a return to the spirit of repentance on a national scale and to that of the spirit of *forgiveness* generally. Solzhenitsyn's geopolitics is, therefore, geared to a small-scale economy, an ecology suffused with respect for creation, an abandonment of 'economic progress'.

4. THE FULLNESS

These three 'No's' did not appear all at once. We can, however, see that they follow on from each other. With each successive 'No', Solzhenitsyn has lost followers, because his demands grew in proportion to his self-discovery. He says as much in *Oak and the Calf*: 'It is time to speak out more and more clearly and to go more and more deeply. This will inevitably entail the loss of readers, people alive now who place their hope in their heirs. But it is heart-breaking to lose even those nearest ones.' I think that we do well to note that, beyond all the polemics and what we have to acknowledge to be sometimes excessive hagiographies, our age has been fascinated by Solzhenitsyn's progressive 'disclosure', has been constantly struck by his complete acceptance of the supreme risk (everything he says he says in the face of death, with 'his death in his cheek') and at the same time by the overflowing joy of this fighter. This exultant joy derives at once from an acute sense of the fullness of earthly existence (nature, man, suffering, camp and even the worst refuse of humanity) and from an intense faith in providence. This born fighter, this genial tactician of dissidence is also an active and abandoned contemplative. There is no doubt in him something of the simple jubilation of the great creative spirits, who experience no doubt, who give themselves up to the superabundance of their creative energy. But there is also the full peace of the fighter armed with faith. Solzhenitsyn may have a contemplative, medieval face, but it is inseparable from another, alight with energy and struggle.

Having brought back an energetic, uncluttered Russian language, he is at present engaged in writing a big historical novel, *The Red Wheel*, in which he is trying to locate the nodal points of Russia's destiny, those moments when in his opinion Russia lost—or, rather, obscured—its soul. This massive historical inquiry in which he runs the risk of making historical mistakes, stokes controversy amongst the Russian émigrés. In the West it is more the subordinate place which he assigns to democracy (democracy for what?) that feeds the debate. He breaks taboos in all spheres, and yet his influence in our times is great. He has brought back a certain sense of human and historical integrity. He has found the resources to think through the leviathan of the gulag, not only without sinking into dereliction (like a Chalamov) but transforming it joyously into a way of salvation.

The secret of this fullness is clearly that he has thought of the gulag as a second Golgotha. This was a difficult, almost an insurmountable intellectual task to tackle because it could not afford to topple into a pious metaphor or to cheapen the moan of a humanity crushed by our century in the name of an ideology of happiness. 'Nobody, no, nobody, set out to torture us. Our guardians' conduct is perfectly rational. All the same, here we are, like the first Christians, crouching in the cage and they put salt on our wounded tongues. . . . Did they really crucify Christ between the thieves because Pilate wanted to humiliate him? No, it was the times that demanded this: there had to be a crucifixion, there was only one Golgotha, and the time was pressing. *And he was reckoned with transgressor.*' (*The Gulag Archipelago* II, 1.)

Solzhenitsyn's overriding purpose has, therefore, been—and will no doubt continue to be—to reintegrate the century of industrialised torture into the perpetually unfinished economy of salvation.

Translated by Iain McGonagle

Notes

1. This is a collection of articles by Solzhenitsyn and his ideological companions, E. Barabanov and I. Chafarevitch. The collection was prepared before the events of 1974, but by the time it actually appeared, the initiator of the collection, Solzhenitsyn, had already been exiled to the West. Three important articles of his are to be found here: 'As Breathing and Consciousness Return'; 'Repentance and Self-Limitation in the Life of Nations'; and 'The Smatterers'.

Ed Grace

The Churches Behind a
United Europe

IN SO FAR as the European Economic Community (EEC) is today the world's richest commercial grouping, the economic-political unification of Europe and the direction of its future evolution, positively or negatively touches all peoples, be they First or Third World, easterners or westerners or non-aligned, be they Christian, Moslems or Non-Believers. The role of the Christian churches in the EEC's unification and evolution must therefore be looked into with care. Partial analyses which tend above all to skip over hard economic structures and the biting issues of today can lead Christians to have a 'gnostic' awareness of Europe, detrimental for preaching the gospel and celebrating living Eucharists capable of providing critical judgment on the direction of the structural transformations taking place in Europe and in the world. (Due to personal background, emphasis will be placed on the Catholic Church, although not exclusively.)

1. THE UNDERLYING MOTIVATION BEHIND THE UNIFICATION OF EUROPE

'The European Community of Coal and Steel' was set up on 18 April 1951 due largely to the effort of Jean Monnet, who was also its first president, and the French minister, Schuman. This institution had real inter-European power and for this reason its charter was considered as revolutionary with respect to preceeding multi-European institutions. The central objective of the organisation was to place the whole of the French-German steel and coal production under a common, overriding authority in a company open to the participation of other European countries. Belgium, Holland, Italy and Luxembourg joined the French and Germans in the initiative.[1] Already at this stage, the democratic election of a European Parliament had been provided for to create greater integration; it took twenty-nine long years for the election to be held.[2] The Treaty of Rome in 1957 marked both the official birth of the European Economic Community and the creation of the European Atomic Agency.[3] Within a relatively short period, the EEC became the first commercial power in the world. In 1972 its exports represented 27·6 per cent of the western world market while that of the USA was 16·9 per cent. In 1973 Denmark, Great Britain and Ireland became members. This rapid economic development was due in large part to: (1) a constant policy of common external tariffs against foreign competition; (2) progressive liberalisation of the internal

19

commerce of the European community;[4] (3) the international monetary stability based on the dollar; and (4) the *low cost* of energy and raw materials.[5]

Today this specifically means a mixture of agricultural protectionism, import tariffs against advanced technology products of Japan and the USA, increased investments in research and *advantageous cost* for energy and raw materials. In addition, a planned, stable importing of elementary industrial products and agricultural goods from the Third World needs to be worked out in order to provide these latter with credit or cash reserves to buy European goods; the reduction of the cost of 'subsistence goods' must also be elaborated in order to keep down manufacturing costs and increase competitiveness.[6]

An element of continual difficulty for strengthening the key, European based, industrial sector has been the general tendency of national governments to exercise their sovereignty with respect to economic decisions, thus creating difficulties for the free movement of European capital on a continental level, not to mention the creation of a single continental currency or one central govenment as in the USA. Hence the need for additional political integration.[7]

This growing, if not urgent need of European-based capital to have a collective, independent, European-centred policy can be seen, for example, in relationship to Middle East oil without which the European economy would come to a grinding halt with all its internal, social-political consequences.[8]

In short, the present, political-economic unification underway among western European countries is not a Christian Church project anymore than was the feudal economy of the middle ages which lead to the fragmentary 'princedoms' and 'bishopdoms' of that epoch. Given that this political-economic transformation is an evolving fact, the real questions, therefore, are: (1) Are the churches for or against this unification?; (2) Do they accept or oppose the present political structures?; (3) Are they tending to legitimise, change or condition the underlying economic structures?; (4) Are the churches 'Christianising' Europe or trying to be Christian in Europe today?

2. THE CHRISTIAN CHURCHES AND THE UNIFICATION OF EUROPE

In almost all the documents available (both Catholic and Protestant), the vision of a 'united Europe' goes beyond the nine nations of the EEC and is extended to all European countries. This concept was already present in an earlier document of the Belgium bishops (23 November 1976). 'Values which are dear to us have continued to grow and develop through the centuries and within the dimensions of Europe, from the Urals to the Atlantic.'[9] The German Evangelical Church has a similar view[10]. 'The European community is only a part of Europe. The European community must remain open to contact and collaboration with the people of Eastern Europe. Europe does not end at the Elbe.'[11] Extending the concept of Europe beyond the western section was also evident in the highly representative statement of the European Bishops' Conferences on 19 April 1979. 'Without forgetting this concern for Europe in its East-West integrity, it is in this same perspective that we must today view the occasion of the forthcoming . . . elections . . .'[12]

This invitation to Catholics to work for a 'wider Europe' than that of the EEC was already expressed by Paul VI in 1966. Today that generic statement has taken on concrete dimensions such as the active participation of Vatican diplomacy at the Helsinki Conference and their working for its continuation. The new bishop of Rome, likewise, strongly insists on a broad vision of Europe; 'it runs along the Ural mountains' and everything west of it. It can be regarded as a spacious peninsula of the Euro-Asiatic continent. This call for a broader vision of Europe is very important for future dialogue, but in relation to EEC unification, it is a sort of indirect support, here-and-now. In fact, the general tone of the documents all favour this process of unification in act.

3. THE CHRISTIAN CHURCHES, DEMOCRACY AND HUMAN RIGHTS IN EUROPE

As to the role of democratic elections and parliamentary government in European unification, the Catholic bishops clearly stand in favour of the present state of the question: 'As bishops of the Common Market we ask all Catholics to feel responsibly involved in the forthcoming election of the European Parliament and to understand the importance so as to be able to participate as Christians with full intelligence in the problems of Europe.'[13] Given past European history, especially with respect to Germany and Italy, this call to active participation in democracy should be judged positively. The bishops of Wales and England go a step further in their pastoral letter of 25 March 1979 and make voting a Christian duty except when, according to one's conscience, not voting is seen as the only morally correct response.[14]

The text of the German Evangelical Church is even more explicit on the importance of democracy; they see it as a condition for a united Europe and tie it in with human rights. 'The European Community must be a democratically mature community, in which respect for human dignity and freedom are a norm. . . .'[15] On the human rights' issues, the European Catholic bishops also express concern and list some rights they believe must be guaranteed 'in the new Europe': 'right to life, the rights of children before and after birth, women's rights, those of the family, refugees' rights, workers' rights and in particular those of foreign workers.'[16] This concern takes on a rather critical tone when the bishops ask: 'Will these fundamental values be taken into account?'[17] The German Evangelical Church is no less critical; for them 'the question remains open if in this manner, that is with the unification of States and peoples, the aim of assuring peace on earth, making justice more believable among men and of increasing help to the poor will be reached?'[18]

As a whole it can thus be said that while the European Christian churches are favourably disposed towards democratically elected parliamentary government, they have not 'Christianised' it. In addition, they have expressed concern for human rights and are conscious that democratic elections and European unification do not *per se* guarantee either peace or establish justice.

4. THE CHRISTIAN CHURCHES AND THE EUROPEAN ECONOMIC STRUCTURES

Given that the driving impulses behind European unification have been primarily economic, it is essential to see where the Christian churches stand on the Western European economy as structured today. Do they give it a Christian baptism? On the basis of the 1979 document signed by the ten bishops' conferences directly concerned, the answer is 'No'. Do they propose a socialistic structured economy? The answer is 'No'. Of course, in any given situation, silence is consent. Notwithstanding this tacit consent, they do lay down some conditions. One very important condition is concern for economic justice towards the Third World; this is a first step away from the tacit justification of economic, neo-colonialism. 'We retain,' they state, 'that Europeans are responsible towards the other countries and above all for Third World countries which must be treated as equals and not as welfare recipients, much less as exploited.' 'When a large part of the population continues to be under-nourished . . . sometimes dying of hunger, is it not a scandal that the industrialised countries live in opulence?'[19]

It is very clear from this that European churches are aware of present economic imbalances and the resulting injustices which the Christian message cannot tolerate. These are lucid principles while somewhat vague in application. The Belgium National Bishops' Conference was more specific—always within the optic of the present economic structures—'the industrial and commercial companies, the cultural and health organisations will be set up in such a way as to give the first place to the human person'.[20] It is really questionable, especially when expanded to a Third World dimension, if the present economic system can meet these conditions.

In fact, such Church-based organisations as the French Justice and Peace Commission are calling for a new economic order. 'The expression "New International Economic Order",' they explain, 'was first mentioned in the non-aligned nations meeting in Algeria in 1973.' 'This Third World request for a new international economic order,' they argue, 'is acceptable because the "present order" does not meet numerous legitimate needs of the peoples. . . .'[21] The Commission has taken a step further than the European bishops; in fact, it is not clear how far the bishops intend to go towards pressing for Third World economic rights. In any case, the Commission and the bishops use similar examples. 'Hunger and famine rage among some people while the technical know-how exists which would permit the development of sufficient agricultural production. Technical know-how used by others has allowed for the accumulation of stock and at times the destruction or the waste of food.'[22]

In a like manner, Douglas Hyde, speaking on EEC unification, surely reflects the opinion of many concerned European and world Christians. He believes 'there is something indecent about men confronted with stocks of food in a world of want, wondering how best they can dispose of them without bringing down the price of the home market.' 'What more could one do if one were deliberately setting out to erode basic human values?'[23]

Bishop Hengsbach speaking in the name of the German Bishops' Conference evaluates the issue differently. He does not call for a new international economic order but sees the European elections as offering the possibility to reinforce 'a policy in favour of the market economic system' and 'the right to private property', 'fundamental rights which are expressed in Catholic social doctrine'. He urges Catholics to 'take up responsibility in the organisation of the future Europe' in order to reach these goals and to reinforce 'free Europe against the threat coming from the communist world'.[24] Other varying positions with regard to the underlying economic system are held by Christians, for example, Christians for Socialism. Let it suffice here to keep in mind that the issue is (1) non-dogmatic; (2) vital when considering solutions to world justice and human rights; and (3) notwithstanding the joint 1979 bishops' document, conflicting positions exist between, and most likely within, the national bishops' conferences. And given the extreme importance of the issue and the interests involved, these differences will probably emerge in time and could even explode in a moment of crisis.

5. EUROPEAN UNIFICATION, EUROPEAN CULTURE AND THE CHRISTIAN MESSAGE

Due to its practical ramification in producing critical thought, no issue will be more crucial in determining the churches' capacity to speak out on human rights and economic justice within the EEC unification than the position it takes with respect to culture, European culture and culture in general. For example, even the highly nuanced Belgium bishops in their document on Europe tend to identify the *kerygma* of the Christian message with European culture when they state that 'in as much as we are European we have a vision of the person and of society in which the humanism and wisdom which comes from the gospel integrate one another reciprocally'.[25] Such a statement tends to 'sanctify' some vague European culture, make it superior, and detach it from its historical structural evolution; in short, render it uncriticable. But, for example, is it not a historical fact that a greater part of European humanism came from the rediscovery of classical Greek and Roman culture? Is not the gospel originally from Semitic culture? The 1977 European bishops' statement on Europe is similar. It almost completely identifies the Christian message with the European interpretation and application of it; they state that 'the Christian tradition belongs essentially to Europe'.[26] Naturally the Christian message launched through a Jewish, Middle East culture has had to be wrestled out within a European culture, giving rise to theologies and movements and institutions which tried (they need be judged critically) to respond authentically to the particular economic, social, political cultural situation of their epochs. But if this idea that 'Christian tradition belongs essentially to Europe' is not overcome, the equally authentic wrestling of other Christians, as, for example, Third World contributions to the faith, especially in the area of justice, can be termed as not essentially Christian and set aside in the European consciousness.

For this reason the 1979 document of the European bishops represents a marked evolution in this vital question; it lays a basis, although not developed in the document, for a continual and universal opening towards all cultures. 'Created in the image of God, the human person has in him/herself spiritual values.' This same principle, opening towards all cultures, was expressed during a talk on 'Europe and Saint Benedict' given by Bartolomeo Sorge, editor of La Civiltà Cattolica (a cultural review considered near the pope). 'The Christian message,' he states, 'is not tied to any particular form of human culture or political, economic or social system and is not identifiable with one of the other ideologies or military blocks.'[27] Such a clear statement coming from the Vatican area is an important evolution. No one culture is superior, hence Third World theologies need not be measured for European purity but for authentic wrestling with the Christian message in their own culture. In his same talk, however, Sorge goes on to state something that needs special attention as it is pertinent to justice in the EEC and to the relationship between being Christian and Christianising. Sorge maintains that Saint Benedict 'realised a synthesis between pagan culture and Christian culture which paved the way for "Medieval Christianity" '. The peoples were united 'in the same faith and culture and by a concept of work and an economic order made to the measure of man'.[28] Besides contradicting his previous statement on culture, Sorge seemingly falls back into 'sanctifying', this time a whole historical period. Such a 'Christianising' statement seems to present the Catholic Church as having a sort of built-in economic programme made to the measure of man. This is not only historically incorrect, it is misleading and could hinder Christian justice today by presenting an uprooted, abstract vision rather than analysing the fruits of EEC unification.

In the first place, the feudal economy of that epoch was not created by the Church. It was the result of the decline of commerce after the loss of access to the Mediterranean trade routes closed by the Saracens. In the resulting static or local economy, the Church—as structure—found itself in a privileged position as land-owner and educated class.[29] As part of the ruling class, it naturally put its stamp on the culture of that period, but as ruling class, not necessarily as driven by the Christian message. Moreover, it is highly doubtful that serfs of the middle ages, deprived of all property rights and the many human rights tied to property (freedom of movement, of marriage, etc.) would consider the middle ages as a period in which the economic order was made to the measure of man. This uncritical depiction of an (any) epoch as idyllic and as coming wholly forth from the gospel is incorrect and detrimental to Christian witness in the EEC. It is not, in part or in whole, the identification of past cultural expressions with the authentic meaning of the gospel message that lie behind recent attacks against theologians who are working to help re-evangelise Europe (and the contemporary world) by confronting the Christian faith with modern European and world culture(s).

Certainly in the process of European unification, past Christians and their creative secular initiatives—such as the development of the Slovak alphabet—can be held up as examples by the churches, but always and only within their global historical context.

If the cultural option to avoid uprooting the past is not made, the churches run the risk of *creating* a 'gnostic' understanding of Christian faith rendering it incapable of 'incarnation' today, *of forming* a closed mentality in many well-intentioned Christians and hence of *slowing down* the efforts of those Christians struggling with the economic transformations in order to create a new 'Slovak alphabet' which will open Europe to be a protagonist of world justice; and of *side-tracking* the European bishops' cultural clarifications, key to a Eucharist which can cut into the burning problems of justice emerging from the evolving process of EEC unification.

Notes

1. A. Caruso 'L'Italia Nell'Europa Unità' *La Civiltà Cattolica* 3095 (2 July 1979) p. 492.

2. G. Rulli 'Le Elezioni Dirette Per Il Parlamento Europeo' *La Civiltà Cattolica* 3097 (7 July 1979) p. 89.

3. Caruso in the article cited in note 1, at p. 492.

4. A. Fonseca 'Verso L'Unità Monetaria Europea' *La Civiltà Cattolica* 3074 (15 July 1978) p. 134.

5. *Ibid*. pp. 135-138.

6. *Ibid*. pp. 142-143.

7. *Ibid*. p. 147.

8. While there are strong democratically elected political forces in Europe working to evolve a socialist economy, none of these deny that the European economy is dependent on commerce having few natural resources.

9. 'The Vocation of Europe', Belgium Bishops' Conference, 23 November 1976, *Il Regno* 7 (1977) p. 172.

10. 'German Evangelical Church Declaration' 21 October 1978, *IDOC-Internazionale* 1-2 (1979) pp. 90-91.

11. Karol Wojtyla 'Frontiers of Europe' *The Tablet* (9 June 1979) pp. 547-548.

12. 'United Europe, Occasion of Brotherhood Among the Peoples', Bishops of the European Community, *IDOC-Internazionale*, 1-2, 1979, p. 90.

13. *Ibid*. p. 91.

14. 'Pastoral Letter of the Bishops of Wales and England', 31 March 1979.

15. 'German Evangelical Church Declaration', cited in note 10, at p. 93.

16. 'Occasion . . .', cited in note 12, at p. 91.

17. *Ibid*. p. 91.

18. 'German Evangelical Church Declaration', cited in note 10, at p. 95.

19. 'United Europe, Occasion . . .', *ibid*. at p. 90.

20. 'The Vocation of Europe', cited in note 9, at p. 173.

21. 'Policy for a New International Economic Order' *Il Regno* 9 (1977) p. 232.

22. *Ibid*. p. 233.

23. Douglas Hyde 'Can the EEC be Christian?' *The Month* (May 1979) p. 160.

24. *Il Regno* 15 March (1978) p. 105.

25. 'The vocation of Europe' cited in note 9, at p. 172.

26. 'A Word on Europe' *Il Regno* 15 (1977) p. 347.

27. *L'Osservatore Romano* 23 March (1980) p. 3.

28. *Ibid*. p. 3.

29. Henri Pirenne *Economic and Social History of Medieval Europe* (Histoire du Moyen Age) (New York 1936) pp. 6-15.

René Laurentin

The Charismatic Movement: Prophetic Renewal or Neo-Conservatism?

TO PUT an article on the charismatic renewal in the context of an issue devoted to neo-conservatism is to court the danger of poisoning the well from the very start—at least wherever conservatism has a pejorative connotation. We must, therefore, begin by exercising the mythic and emotive associations of this term.

Conservation is one of life's essential functions. Ecology (which has taken over from progress in prestige-value since the early Seventies) is the conservation of nature. The Christian faith, which consists in the faithful transmission of a revelation essentially given once and for all, also depends on a vital conservation, on a spiritual ecology. So to think of any concern to conserve as conservatism, backwardness or deviation is to betray a naïve Manicheism. The real problem is: What do we have to conserve? How are we to conserve without choking what is essential for life? How can we combine this conservation with progress and the evolution that is part of human historicity? The study of the charismatic renewal enables us to illustrate this problem in a very topical way.

1. THE CHARISMATIC RENEWAL: AN INNOVATION

The charismatic renewal[1] is, above all, the product of a daring innovation. For the fact is that this Catholic movement drew its initial inspiration (baptism in the Spirit and the charism) from Protestant settings—or, more particularly, from the enthusiastic and even sometimes sectarian movement known as Pentecostalism.

The critical date here is January 1967, in Pittsburgh. The first four Catholics to be 'baptised in the Spirit'[2] were not thought of as being particularly conservative or formalistic. They were seekers who had responded sympathetically to the wave of criticism unfurled in the United States by John XXIII. The moral they had drawn from Vatican II was that they had to become socially involved. But their efforts at social or even political work had dissipated rather than reinforced their faith. They felt the need for some *source* (John 7:37-39; and see 4:14). It was at this moment that they read David Wilkerson's book *The Cross and the Switchblade*.[3] This pastor had experienced in the pouring out of the Spirit a deep impulse which had wrenched him out of a well-established parish life and taken him into a dangerous and fruitful apostolate in New York's underworld of thieves. These four Catholics would not have dreamed of asking for initiation at the hands of Pentecostalists, so they sought and found it amongst Episcopalian charismatics, who were very close to Catholicism but who had welcomed and assimilated the 'Pentecostalist' experience. This is the way in which what was at first called simply Catholic Pentecostalism came into being on 20 January 1967, as a result of prayer and the laying of hands on the first two founders: a conversion, a liberation of vital forces, and a sudden flowering of charisms quite forgotten in the Catholic Church, beginning with speaking in tongues, characteristic of Pentecostalism, but also including prophecy (in the sense of inspired words, pronounced in the name of God), the gift of healing, etc.

All this represented a daring innovation, and was experienced as such. When people first began speaking in tongues at Notre Dame, Indiana, USA, in February 1967, an old missionary, who had known the proselytism of certain anti-Catholic Pentecostalist groups asked sententiously: 'When are you going to leave the Church?' Those who were taken over by this élan did not feel any disaffection themselves, on the contrary. Nevertheless the daring of this ecumenism and of this borrowing, the unwanted and provocative novelty of baptism in the Spirit (was it a second baptism?), the charisms (above all the speaking in tongues) and the words spoken to the whole assembly by any ordinary person in the name of God, the free improvisation of prayer, astounded and even shocked people.

All movements of the Spirit have surprised and shocked people, from the time of the Acts of the Apostles (2:13; 26:24), when the Church of Pentecost was referred to as a *hairesis*, with the double connotation of heresy and sect (Acts 24:14; 28:22). For layfolk to exercise the charism of 'deliverance' seemed to be trespassing on the functions of the exorcists and so to be an aberration. More generally, the leadership of laypeople in this movement, the authority of charisms which they had, seemed to be subversive. That a bishop, or even a cardinal, who had entered the movement, should have allowed women and non-Catholics to exercise the laying of hands on them seemed to be an aberration. It was no good for 'Catholic Pentecostalists' to reply by saying that the gesture had been polyvalent from the beginning and had no sacramental import or intention and that it was an invocation to ask the Spirit in its serene wisdom to grant that the grace of baptism given once and for all be allowed to live, the way Catholics reacted to these unusual novelties was reminiscent of the hen which had hatched ducklings.

It is very much to the credit of the bishops of the United States, where this movement was born, that despite apprehensions (and inevitable ambiguities and excesses), they should have discerned in it a movement of the Spirit that was authentically Catholic, in the sense of something genuinely universal and not particularist. Ten years earlier such a movement would have been immediately condemned out of hand.

2. FACTORS MAKING FOR TRADITION FROM WITHIN

How is it that this risky ecumenical experience should now have come to be dubbed 'conservative'? The reason is to be found in an essential and inherent characteristic of the movement: it inspires a return, not only to the Bible but to the Christian tradition in all its varied forms.

(a) Rediscovery of the plenitude of tradition

This is one of the facts that has most struck me amongst charismatic groups in a good dozen countries which I have visited. I have heard one of the French leaders of this movement, Père de Monléon, throw out to many audiences a challenge which has never been taken up: 'Cite me a single Christian value which is not experienced and lived out in the renewal; anything from devotion to the Trinity to the veneration of the saints, from ecumenism to the recitation of the rosary, from fasting to feasting.'

It is true that all this and more is to be found in authentic groups of the renewal, each one reinventing from within varied characteristics which together make up a whole that it is not easy to classify as either traditionalist or progressive: the taste for the apostolate but also for withdrawal, even for the eremitical life; the sense of God's gracious working but also of sin; of joy but also of penance; attraction towards the sacraments (and above all the Eucharist) but also to all manner of particular devotions. In other words, what we find is integrity without integrism, that is to say, without narrowness, passion or affectation—at least where the renewal is lived out authentically, which, in my experience, in more cases than not it is.

In this way, Christianity is breaking out again with a variety going as far as contrast. What strikes one in these communities of the renewal is the assurance—and the joy—with which everybody chooses his state of life, whether it be celibate or married. I have heard a young man at Ann Arbor say quite simply at an agapé held after the wedding of one of the young people in the community: 'I was very happy for them both but I could not see myself in their place. So far as my own future is concerned, I saw myself in the place of the priest who officiated at the wedding.'

Many unhappy couples, sometimes on the brink of divorce, have seen their first love reflower and have found the strength to rebuild their home as a result of allowing the Spirit to be poured into their lives. By the same token, priests suffering from a crisis of identity have gained a second wind and fruitfulness in their ministry. Charismatic retreats for priests have to date drawn more than 1,000 priests in the USA.

If such a resurgence of tradition is bringing practically all the forms of the past back to life, especially those which had seemed to be outworn, or at least on the decline—the rosary, veneration of the saints, confession and spiritual direction, etc.—it is not a matter of some archaism or a manic return to ancient forms. It is, on the contrary, a question of a rediscovery, a revitalisation, and, moreover, of such an occurrence from within, by way of attraction and creativity. To cite only one example, the communities that are monastic in character, which are growing up spontaneously within the renewal, including celibate ones, do not adopt the rules of the religious communities that have emerged in the past ten centuries. They rediscover the rule of life from within. And if they do sometimes return to the traditional rules, it is by way of convergence and not of borrowing. This is true of the 'charters of alliance' worked out by the two celibate communities, a Brotherhood and a Sisterhood, of Ann Arbor, and the communities of various monastic types in France, at Grenoble, Montpellier ('Theophanie' in Montpellier, 'Lion de Juda' in Cordes, etc.).

So far as the rediscovery of the traditional faith is concerned, the process is reminiscent of the experience of converts who have come to Christianity from outside. I think, for example, of Marie-Alphonse Ratisbonne, the young Jewish banker, anti-Christian by family tradition, who came to the Christian faith all of a sudden through a vision of the Virgin Mary which he had in Rome on 20 January 1842: 'She never said a word, but I understood everything,' is the way he summed it all up. When he was being instructed, he seemed to *recognise* all the truths which he had never heard, in the sense that they corresponded in every particular to his expectation. André Frossard and other converts had the same experience of seeming to remember. They found in their instruction, whether theoretical or practical, the very truths of which they had a presentiment; it prompted their joyful adherence: 'That's just how it is. Amen.'

This experience of the outpouring of the Spirit verifies what the New Testament and an authentic pneumatology teaches us about the Holy Spirit. It is a question not of something from without, but of something from within, 'a spring of water welling up to eternal life' (John 4:14; 7:37-39). It does not infuse hackneyed forms or ready-made information, but a light which illuminates the truth objectively transmitted by revelation, an élan which regenerates the forms of Christian life, or promotes creative reinvention. This is the way the Holy Spirit rouses up individuals and groups, in all their historical, geographical, cultural and other diversity. This is the way Christians are identified with Christ, not identically but in a variety of forms and expressions.

This the nature of the experience of the Spirit: every time it has been renewed, from the time of the prophets of the New Testament to our own day, there has been a simultaneous movement of return to the most distant past in revelation and a powerful thrust towards the future of God, the Church and the world. In the Spirit, tradition is not opposed to progress. On the contrary, it is the deepest return to the source that releases the most daring jet towards the future. Francis of Assisi and Vincent de Paul, amongst others, exemplify this truth.

(b) Receiving this Plenitude in Earthen Vessels

Man being what he is, this happy combination comes into being within the limits of human weakness and via the vicissitudes of sin ingrained in our world. So the absoluteness of God and of the Spirit only comes home to us through the relativities of the human condition.

We can note three things that help us to understand how a movement that began by being so novel has tended to become conservative or at least to appear to be.

(i) *The need for obedience*

Charismatic conversion fans the need for strong institutions and obedience. This is strikingly so in the case of classic Pentecostalism. One of them, an American in a smart suit and tie, one day confided to me that the 'shepherd' of his community had a few months before ordered him to cut his hippy beard and long hair. He had done so, and rejoiced in this holocaust which had reinforced his fervour. I asked myself why the leader had made such an issue of so relative a thing. After all, I thought to myself, there was a contrast between the eastern traditions requiring monks to have beards and long hair and the practice of monks in the West shaving their heads. The need for a rule and for obedience is sometimes fed by a relative contrast.

(ii) *Institutional loyalty*

Neo-Pentecostalism, that is to say, the extension of the Pentecostalist experience to the traditional churches—the Anglican in 1958, the Lutheran in 1964 and the Catholic in 1967—is characterised by the loyalty and rigorous fidelity of the charismatics to their respective churches, and all the more so for these particular churches being more traditional.

(iii) *The law of creative life*

Finally, charismatic communities develop in accordance with a general law of all life. Every vital movement creates new forms, after which it is ready to close in on itself and harden. This, according to Bergson, is the law of any vital élan, including a religious élan. An open religion typically evolves into a closed one and then the élan loses momentum and keeps to itself (see H. Bergson, *Les deux sources de la foi et de la religion*, Paris 1932).

This, then, is the way in which an authentic movement of the Spirit, the charismatic renewal, like that of Francis of Assisi and many others before it, can be called traditional and even conservative. This is also why Tertullian, a Montanist and a schismatic, kept a reputation for being a traditionalist.

3. FACTORS MAKING FOR TRADITION FROM WITHOUT

To the factors making for tradition already outlined we must now add other, extrinsic factors tending in the same direction.

(a) Coincidence with the surrounding neo-conservatism

First of all, the charismatic renewal, born at the beginning of 1967, knew its great expansion in the Seventies. This was when tradition (which had been rather jostled aside by the Council) made a come-back against progress, and fidelity against criticism and suspicion. Nor is this a merely religious phenomenon, it is secular and world-wide. The Sixties had been the years of optimism and progressive daring, the era of John XXIII, Kennedy, Krushchev, as the case might be. The Seventies were the time when people realised the limits and the disadvantages of 'progress', and the way in which it could cause men and their environment to disintegrate. It was in this spirit that the Club of Rome replaced the ideal of maximum growth with that of zero growth, whilst the ecological movement caught on throughout the world. We do not need to insist on this since it is one of the themes of the present issue, but we do have to stress that this powerful conservative current did influence the evolution of the charismatic renewal. This is not the place in which to detail the pros and cons of this coincidence: the way in which it, on the one hand, corrected excesses and deviations, safeguarded order and balance, and, on the other hand, muffled creativity and the spiritual élan.

(b) Pressure to integrate into the Institution

A second major factor is that the charismatic renewal as a movement born from an experience exterior to Catholicism was subject to many pressures to integrate itself into it, and on that account to sacrifice its innovative and unconventional sides in favour of Catholic forms. These latter were praised, developed and encouraged, whilst the others were criticised, devalued and discouraged.

Such an integration is necessary. Christian groups which have become possessed of a new idea and then gone it alone have often ended up by breaking with the Church and breaking up within themselves. But we have to reckon with a well-known sociological law: every innovation group, like mutants in biology, is subject to the bio-mechanism of rejection and absorption in accordance with the dilemma of assimilation or exclusion. Exclusion can be stimulated by a process of mutual activity in which repression provokes the sub-group to rebel, and vice versa. It is in this way that the Inquisition went so far as to burn Savanarola who criticised the moral deviations of the Holy See (which were apparent enough in any case). The alternative is for the charismatic sub-group to submit. But in that case there is a risk that it will sink back into conventionality, platitude and surliness, which are just what it wanted to escape.

In the case of the charismatic renewal, this integration took place in exceptionally favourable circumstances, at a time when the episcopacy, having been opened up by the Council and overwhelmed by innumerable conflicts, was particularly receptive to new experiences. The new Pentecostal impulse was not rejected by the Catholic Church as it had been by the Methodists at the beginning. The obedience and docility of the charismatic groups facilitated this integration—but at the price of a certain deadening of creativity and of the charismatic élan. In order to be accepted, the movement changed its original name from Catholic Pentecostalism (which was in fact rather a shock for Pentecostalists as well as for Catholics) to charismatic renewal. There were, however, Catholic theologians to criticise this new label. 'This label is an abuse,' they said, 'because no movement has a corner in charisms.' On this principle, however, Ignatius of Loyola should have been forbidden to call the Order he founded (in a charismatic élan which was suspected at the time of being contaminated by the famous *Alhumbrados*) the Society of Jesus, because Jesus belongs to everybody. Nobody in the sixteenth century, however, criticised St Ignatius for having 'made a corner' in Jesus.

This docility attenuated the charismatic and ecumenical thrust of the movement and stimulated its conservative side.[4] The blame for this development must not be put purely and simply on authority—which held a tight rein in some countries and a loose one in others—but on the general body of the Church which was rather ironic about the 'charismatics', and particularly on the clergy and theologians, traditionally allergic to enthusiastic movements, in the way the scribes and Pharisees (admirable men to whom history is today doing justice . . .[5]) were in regard to Jesus.

These influences making for the levelling out of charisms did remedy the various risks of illuminism, sectarianism, emotionalism, etc., which had been evoked with such force during the first years of the movement. But an excessive prudence did also prevent many groups from having the courage of their charisms and of their spiritual adventure. Many of them died of boredom and moodiness. From the point of integration which we have reached now, it would seem on balance that the risks are less on the side of excess than on that of institutionalisation and levelling out. For some excesses are fruitful and correct themselves, whilst lethargy and mediocrity end in sterility. All of which is not to underestimate the tricky way such movements have to pick between these two risks, as between Scylla and Charybdis.

4. COMPENSATORY REACTIONS AGAINST CONSERVATISM

A certain conservatism, therefore, may indeed have dominated the charismatic renewal (to different degrees, in different countries and in situations which have to be judged on their own), it may have diminished the speaking of tongues and regenerated Catholic practices, made some groups less open to Protestants, and emphasised the mystical at the expense of social and political involvement. This whole tendency has, however, been powerfully counter-balanced from within the movement itself.

This counter-balancing has been particularly marked in the matter of social involvement. The leaders of the renewal, the core groups of which work in a collegial and not in a hierarchical manner, have organised many meetings to promote this aspect of things, and especially in Latin America. It is to this end that Cardinal Suenens has secured the collaboration of Helder Camara.[6]

This concern to be socially committed has emerged essentially from within the movement itself, sometimes to a very pronounced degree. This is the way in which a movement of extraordinary activity has been born in El Paso and Juarez, the two large frontier towns built back to back on either side of the Rio Grande, between Mexico and the USA, and all their activity is catalysed by the giving of material, spiritual and fraternal help to those who are hungry, in an astonishing proliferation of charisus, and, it would seem, of miracles: healings and multiplications of loaves are not considered to be myths and memories of a spent past in these communities. They are part of the humble day-to-day experience of the poor. Those who live these experiences understand that the miracles of the gospel are not mythological inventions—although they do assume a symbolic force—but arise out of the shock of the material and social realities of daily life. They at once bewilder and fulfil both the illiterate Mexicans who count on their fingers and Americans with their pocket calculators who often find that there is *too much* left at the end of the distribution although in general the penury is such that insufficiency and waste are the rule.[7]

5. BY WAY OF CONCLUSION

In theory, the balance between conservation and progress, between institution and charism, goes without saying. In practice, it is normal and problem-free where the Spirit blows. Tension and antagonism arise only where this is not the case. This is the problem of the charismatic renewal, as it has been for all movements of this type from the beginnings of the Church. This is why the Spirit must always be rebeginning.

There is nothing new in this. Elias, Elisha, the first prophetic group attested by the Bible, provoked distrust, irony and repression. In most cases, they were silenced. Amos was expelled (Amos 7:12-13), Jeremiah imprisoned (Jer. 38:1-13). They were told: 'You shall not prophesy' (Amos 2:11-12), 'See not' (Isa. 30:10; and see Jer. 11:21; Nehemiah 9:30).[8] This objective was finally achieved and so a cry went up within the Bible itself to the effect that there are 'no more prophets in Israel'. In this regard, the charismatic renewal has met with a more open welcome than the prophets of the Bible, the spiritual movements of the middle ages or the *Alhumbrados* of the sixteenth century: groups which are difficult to judge since they are known principally through their critics. The Holy Spirit has a great deal to do in order to maintain the balance between conservation and progress, tradition and inspiration.[9]

Translated by John Maxwell

Notes

1. R. Laurentin *Catholic Pentecostalism* (London 1977).
2. The experience of being baptised in the Spirit is attested in the New Testament, where this expression denotes either Christian initiation in a global sense (1 Cor. 12:13; and see John 3:5; 1 John 5:6, 8) or else the most striking (the charismatic) aspect of the manifestation of the Spirit (Acts 11:15-16; 19:2). For the baptism in the Spirit and the charisms, see the book cited in note 1, chapter 3.
3. Spire Books, Old Toppan, N.J., 1970, (London 1967).
4. Initiatives taken to ensure the integration of the movement into the Church have generally proved stronger than those taken in an ecumenical interest, when these have been in conflict. To take one example, in 1964 Ralph Martine had, during the annual convention held at Notre Dame, Indiana, prophetically outlined a programme of an ecumenism of charisms. What he had said in substance was that the renewal had made him admit his fidelity to the Catholic Church. What they now had to do was to go ahead and work boldly for unity. This programme had a great immediate impact but was subsequently neutralised. In France, where the movement has preserved a rare balance of tradition and creativity, the idea of an ecumenical meeting at Pentecost in 1976 was replaced by that of a meeting at Lourdes, a Marian shrine which as such would tend to put off Protestants. The most ecumenical charismatic groups expressed their regret by abstaining. An ecumenical meeting has, however, been scheduled for 1982.
5. On 2 March 1980, Cardinal Etchegarry, president of the French Episcopal Conference, published a declaration endorsing the historic rehabilitation of the Pharisees, who have so often

been misrepresented in the past. This courageous declaration does not do away with the problem presented by the gospel. Even if we must indeed rehabilitate the 'Pharisees of the heart', the subtle and forceful denunciation of the scribes and the Pharisees in the gospel nowadays touches theologians and clerics who resemble them.

6. See L. J. Suenens and Helder Camara *Renouveau dans l'Esprit et service de l'homme* (Documents de Malines 3, Brussels 1979). Cardinal Suenens may have reacted forcefully against certain sorts of charismatic and ecumenical activity, but he has done so within the context of a fundamental encouragement of ecumenism, which he has expressed more concretely in his book *Oecumenisme et renouveau charismatique* (Documents de Malines 2, Paris 1978).

7. I am at present preparing a monograph on this astounding evangelical community (which I visited in the summer of 1979), under the probable title *Miracle à El Paso*. The healings raise problems akin to those we discuss and sometimes get bogged down in at Lourdes. It is difficult, even, no doubt, impossible, to establish proofs in a matter governed above all by gratuitousness and where experiment and replicability are out of the question. And this is all the more the case in regard to incidents of multiplication of food, which always happen unexpectedly and mysteriously, and about which I have gathered testimonies reminiscent of those that could have given rise to the stories of the multiplication of loaves in the gospels and which also shock the reasonable reason.

8. See Walter Vogels 'Il n'y aura plus de prophètes' in *Nouvelle Revue Théologique* (1979) 844-859. This article shows how the 'disappearance of the prophets' (who nevertheless remain necessary) takes place, and how people then go on to complain of their absence. This law of the Old Testament now hangs over the churches.

9. What are the rules of conduct needed to solve the problem? We need: to maintain the primacy of faith in the Holy Spirit; to cultivate interior obedience; to cultivate discernment and not yield to rigidity of thought; to judge the tree by its fruit as described in the New Testament.

Peter Hebblethwaite

Is the Polish Church a Model for the Universal Church?

THOUGH THE theme of this article is detatched and objective, it has acquired a special relevance and no doubt a risk of subjectivism in so far as the present pope happens to be Polish. To ask whether the Polish Church is a model for the Church universal is also to ask, implicitly at least, how far the Polish Church is capable of supplying the rest of the Church with the sort of leadership it needs as it moves towards the year 2,000. So long as a Polish pope did not exist—and he was not foreseen, despite the wisdom of hindsight—there was no need to ask the question. Now it has become ineluctable.

So our theme will be not simply the Polish Church and Polish theology but Karol Wojtyla as a representative of both. There is a danger of latent racialism in asking this question, however legitimately proud one may be of a local tradition, one is not necessarily confined in it; and there are ways in which Wojtyla 'escapes' from his Polish background while still being shaped by it. A paradox is involved here: one needs to be both 'rooted' in a local church and at the same time 'open' to the service of the universal Church.

1. THE PARADOX OF BEING ROOTED AND BEING OPEN

There is some evidence to show that Wojtyla is well aware of this paradox. At any rate he has made statements which can be considered either as contradictory or 'dialectical'—and what one decides they are is a matter of some importance. For example, addressing diplomats on 18 October 1978, just two days after his surprise election, John Paul II said that he valued cultural, historical and linguistic differences and regarded such diversity as an enrichment. He then added: 'From now on the particular nature of our country of origin is of little importance; as a Christian, and still more as pope, we are and will be the witnesses of a universal love'. He seemed to be saying that we should disregard the fact that he is a Pole. But then, on 3 June 1979, speaking at Gniezno on the second day of his Polish journey, he used very different language. He spoke of Polish culture which combines Christian inspiration with deeply felt humanistic values. He quoted Adam Mickiewicz, the nineteenth-century romantic poet: 'A civilisation truly worthy of the name must be a Christian civilisation'. And he

33

concluded: 'You are hearing these words from a man who owes his own spiritual formation from the beginning to Polish culture, to its literature, its music, its plastic arts, to the Polish schools, the Polish universities'. He contrived to omit to mention that he had also studied St John of the Cross at the Angelicum University in Rome. The paradox becomes striking: on 18 October 1978 he declares his independence of the Polish tradition; on 3 June 1979 he proclaims his utter dependence on it.

There are various ways of trying to resolve this paradox. The most hopeful is to point to the philosophical work of Wojtyla which was based on Max Scheler interpreting the late, oracular Edmund Husserl. It has a strongly existential sense of the need for human persons to be 'embodied' and therefore 'somewhere'. One is inserted into the human race through a particular culture, and this is a necessary and desirable insertion; but it does not rule out—and may be the condition—of universal service. Only someone who has a strong sense of 'identity' can have the courage to serve the universal good. A disembodied, disincarnated pope would be an impossibility. That the pope should be firmly rooted in Polish culture might turn out to be an advantage: having lived through an experience of the 'periphery', he can recognise the values of the periphery when he finds himself at the centre.

2. THE CONVICTION OF BEING AN EXEMPLARY NATION

However, this optimistic and abstract analysis overlooks one very important point: the Polish Church or the Polish tradition—the two are distinguished only with difficulty—is convinced that it has a universal mission. It believes that its experience, though unique, is also *exemplary*. So inter-twined are Polish theological self-understanding and cultural experience that it is not abusive to look to Polish nineteenth-century literature for evidence. The situation was, from every point of view, melancholy: the Polish State was wiped off the map, being carved up between Austria (relatively benevolent), Prussia (hostile to Polish cultural aspirations) and Russia (vigorous in its repression of national sentiment). The 'State' did not exist; but the 'nation' survived thanks to culture, religion and language. The situation was so desperate that poets like Mickiewicz interpreted the Polish experience in the light of Christ's Passion. He compared the partition of Poland in 1795 to Christ's first day in the tomb, while the bloody crushing of the revolt of 1831 was the second day. Resurrection and hope lay somewhere ahead, dimly perceived. Poland's twentieth-century experience seemed to confirm this identification. After uneasy independence, Poland was once again partitioned and subjected to régimes more brutal than anything the nineteenth century had known. Independence was finally recovered, but with a régime which Poles had not sought and which depended in large measure, on geo-politics: the Soviet Union was the 'friendly neighbour' to the East, while the 'West' had failed to honour its undertakings towards Poland.

Once one begins to look at the history of a nation in Messianic terms and to identify its atrocious sufferings with the Passion of Christ, then the whole of history has to be seen as the unfolding of a mysteriously providential design. Wojtyla shares in this tradition. It was therefore natural that he should ask why, in 1978, he was elected pope against all expectations. This was his theme in his first major sermon on his return to Poland on 2 June 1979. His answer took the form of a series of questions: 'Have we not the right to think that Poland has today become the land of a specially responsible witness? . . . The right to think that we must come again to this very place, to this land, along this road, to read again the witness of Christ's cross and resurrection?' (Victory Square homily). It was Mickiewicz all over again, with the difference that this time the eschatology was 'realised'. Also in the background of these remarks was the memory of another romantic poet, Juliusz Slowacki, who in 1849 (when Pius IX had fled Rome and taken refuge at Geta) had predicted that the twentieth century would see a Slav pope who, unlike timorous Italians, would not fear sabre thrusts but would lead the nations of the world to a new sense of brotherhood and inter-dependence. The slogan in all Polish revolts had been, 'For our freedom and yours'. National liberation enclosed a universalist role. The election of a Polish pope was the ransom for centuries of persecution, neglect and oppression and the inauguration of a new style of papacy.

3. POLISH SELF-UNDERSTANDING

These historical memories are crucial to contemporary Polish self-understanding. They infiltrate into every sector of the Polish mind. They have resulted in an experience of faith which differs notably from that of Western Europe and the United States (called henceforward, for convenience, the 'West'). The churches of the West have been plagued by guilt-feelings in the last thirty years: they had 'lost the workers', failed to proclaim a relevant message to contemporary urban man, and scandalously exploited the Third World. If the westerners happened to be German, they had the added burden of knowing that their resistance to Hitler had been, despite a few heroic exceptions, feeble.

The Polish Church, on the other hand, had none of these reasons for guilt-feelings. It has not 'lost the workers', despite an official State ideology which declares that they are the vanguard of a new age in which they will be liberated from their superstitious past. It does not feel guilty about the Third World since, apart from the missionaries it has annually exported, it has not been allowed to have any dealings with it. And its record of resistance to Hitlerism is unchallenged: over 2,000 priests died or were executed in concentration camps. Consequently the Polish Church is not oppressed with guilt feelings about its sins of omission or commission.

On the contrary, it has been a victim-Church, and a victim-Church that has somehow, despite terrible odds, survived and flourished. It has had to hope against all hope—twice in the last fifty years. This different experience has produced a different psychology of faith. It issues in a faith that is confident, serene, untrammelled by self-doubt. It is saved from smugness because it has been tested in the crucible of persecution and not found wanting. But in the West all this looks like a form of triumphalism which is unable or unwilling to ask questions, to face inner conflict within the Church, and to accept pluralism as a positive value. The roots of many misunderstandings lie here. They can be uncovered in two stages. What did the Council mean in Poland? And what is the task of theologians in Poland?

4. POLISH REACTIONS TO THE COUNCIL

The Polish bishops did not on the whole welcome the Council. They did not see its necessity. It offered to the world the disedifying spectacle of bishops disagreeing with each other in public. Their entire policy had been based on the unbreakable unity of the episcopate when faced by a communist government. Moreover, the Council proclaimed principles about 'openness to the world' and even learning from it that were not at all congenial in the Polish setting where 'the world' was represented by the Communist Party. Their problem was symbolised when the town council of Wroclaw (formerly the German Breslau) erected a massive statue of Pope John XXIII, the pope of dialogue who could for propaganda purposes be contrasted with the stick-in-the-mud Polish bishops. Moreover, many of the elements which made up Polish Catholicism—its mass pilgrimages, its one-sided Mariology, its doctrinal narrowness—were challenged, implicitly or explicitly, by the Council.

These attitudes were embodied in Cardinal Stefan Wyszyński, twenty years Wojtyla's senior. He was (and is) the Primate, and carried on the tradition of the *inter-rex* (the Primate ruled in the absence of kings). He could not see the relevance of ecumenism to Poland, was uninterested in liturgical reform, believing that Polish peasants had a profound understanding of Latin. The 'kiss of peace', he suggested, turned the church into a salon. The conciliar phrase about *ecclesia semper purigicanda* (a milder form of Luther's *semper reformanda*) he thought highly dangerous, and had it excised from commentaries. In an embattled situation, where loyalty seemed the primary virtue, the Council merely sowed the seeds of confusion. If elsewhere in the Church Catholics rejoiced that the monolith was smashed, this was not so in Poland. Thus the interests of the universal Church appeared to act against the interests of the local church. This was even more true of the subsequent *Ostpolitik* pursued in the pontificate of Paul VI under the general direction of Archbishop (now Cardinal) Agistino Casaroli: the Poles felt that something was going on above their heads directed by people who did not really understand their situation.

One must, however, distinguish between the response of Wyszyński to the Council and that of Wojtyla. The younger man never disagreed publicly with his superior (though the records of the episcopal conference, when published, will show that there were some tough and hard-fought battles). Wojtyla was much more interested in the Council, and found some of its major themes in harmony with his own aspirations. He believed that dialogue should replace confrontation, welcomed liturgical reform, saw the power of religious liberty (as something to be *claimed*), and was committed to ecumenism in so far as is possible in Poland where partners in ecumenical dialogue are hard to find. He also welcomed collegiality and set up in his own diocese a synod that was quite unlike any other diocesan synod: it was essentially a matter of adult education, on a vast scale and over a long period.

Yet despite these (largely unavowed) differences with Wyszyński, Wojtyla's interpretation of the Council remained 'Polish' in its emphasis. This was another reason for later misunderstandings. In the West, to be 'in favour of the Council' implied a whole set of attitudes, hard to define but nevertheless real: an openness to really new questions, a collegial approach to their solution, a leap beyond clericalism, a readiness to learn from the 'world'. In the West, in other words, the Council was experienced as a liberation. It released forces, not all of them predictable.

5. THE POPE'S INTERPRETATION OF THE COUNCIL

This was not quite how Wojtyla, who was sincerely committed to the Council, saw it. In his opening speech to the meeting of cardinals (5 November 1979) he offered a restrictive interpretation of the Council which, so to speak, domesticated and tamed it. He took three themes, *liberty*, *social charity* and *renewal*. The same slogans could be used—have been used—to develop a theology of liberation. But in John Paul's address they were put to very different use. *Liberty* is not the right to do as one pleases, with no regard for the community as a whole. Which is no doubt true, but does not quite legitimate the conclusion that liberty is obedience. *Social charity*, too, is a splendid theme, but in John Paul's presentation it became a way of saying that the 'rich and free' churches of the West ought to come to the aid of those churches that are neither rich nor free. This put the obligation on the First World rather towards the 'Second World' than the 'Third World'. As for *renewal*, it loses all touch with *aggiornamento* and becomes a purely spiritual concept for which the evidence is to be found in a renewed interest in the

Bible and an (alleged) increase of vocations to the priestly and religious life.

In short, in John Paul's interpretation of the Council, it was an end and not a starting-point, it settled questions rather than opening them up, it changed the vocabulary but not the substance, it poured familiar wine into newish bottles. It would be possible to pursue this theme further by an examination of his treatment of 'signs of the times' (which must be interpreted by the magisterium and not by the 'whole Church', as *Gaudim et Spes* suggests) or by his treatment of 'charismatic gifts' (which, yet again, have to be checked out by the magisterium before they can be deemed authentic). It is a defensible view of the Council; but it is also a restrictive and Polish view. In his own context, Karol Wojtyla was undoubtedly 'moderately progressive'; seen in the universal context, he is highly conservative. This is the basis for misunderstandings and *quid pro quos*.

Ignorance of Poland is a chronic condition of the rest of the Church. To be pinned down into a few inaccurate clichés such as 'the Church of silence' or 'a persecuted Church' is galling and produces resentments. 'We are not silent', said a Jesuit theologian in 1971, 'for we have reviews, newspapers and 11,000 pulpits.' 'We are not persecuted,' said Wojtyla in 1972, 'we are harassed.' Yet there was no real excuse for ignorance of the Polish Church. The evidence was there to hand for all who cared to inspect it. In the early 1970s an acute controversy raged in the Polish Church on the role of theologians. Though no one was quite prepared to admit it, the heart of the matter was the place of western theology in Poland. 'We want a Polish theology for Poland,' Wyszyński told the 1972 Congress of Polish Theology, 'written from the standpoint of the East for a community living in the East.' This was a way of repudiating the influence of French, Dutch and German theology which, the cardinal believed, could only do harm in Poland. Even in their own countries, he held, these modish theologians had emptied the churches and contributed powerfully to the process of secularisation. There was no need to import them into Poland. A Polish theologian, A. Zuberbier, replied with some courage that 'there will be a Polish theology only if it is rooted in the theology of the universal Church, only in unity with the universal Church'. The ambivalence of the term 'universal Church' should be noted: it can either mean unity with those Churches that are actively thinking on behalf of the Church as a whole, or unity with the Bishop of Rome.

Wojtyla chose the latter interpretation. His address to the Polish Congress of Theology in 1971, called 'Theology and Theologians in the Post-conciliar Church', foreshadowed future statements on the same topic. For Wojtyla, the Second Vatican Council provided the model for the fruitful collaboration between theologians and pastors. But since then, theologians had presumptuously claimed enhanced status and independence from the magisterium. They were warned against making the Word of God 'an instrument for forcing one's own opinions', reminded that their task was to 'teach and defend the sacred deposit of revelation', and bluntly told that they were subordinate to the bishops who alone have the task of interpreting authentically what is Catholic faith. For good measure, post-conciliar theologians were blamed for sowing the seeds of doubt on such basic doctrines as Christology, the Trinity, the real presence of Christ in the Eucharist, and the indissolubility of marriage. All these themes have recurred in the pontificate. The only surprise is that anyone should have been surprised.

Yet through these dismissive negations, a positive task for theology did manage to emerge. Theology has to re-interpret Catholic tradition in ways more adapted to the contemporary mentality and to contemporary culture. Almost alone among Polish bishops, Wojtyla was insistent on 'the problem of culture': in a State where the mass media and the educational system are the monopoly of one ideological group, it was an essential dimension of the intellectual apostolate. Wojtyla also appreciated that the Council marked a decisive switch from the cosmological to the anthropological approach. Man was at the heart of the conciliar teaching, but he made sense only in the light of Christ, the Second Adam, the one in whom humanity started off afresh on its vocation towards God. This task of re-interpretation can and must be done without 'false irenicism', 'humanism' and even 'secularism'. In Poland, Wojtyla believed—we are still in 1971—these perils had on the whole been avoided; but foreign influences were already making themselves felt. Wojtyla believed that the balance was unequal: Poland imported more theology than it exported.

6. THE CRUCIAL QUESTION

The crucial question—and it involves a value-judgment—is whether the Polish Church's self-understanding is capable of serving the universal Church. The more one stresses the uniqueness of its situation, its cultural conditioning, its historical experience, then the more difficult it becomes to see how it can serve as a model for others. As a contributor to the symphony of the Catholic Church, its heroic role is splendid and not in doubt; as the provider of the conductor of the orchestra, it seems to have limitations. The very qualities which give it strength and cohesion in Poland can become weaknesses when projected on to the international scene. When, for example, the need for a united front becomes a denial of legitimate pluralism, which has the practical consequence of dealing severely with 'dissidents' (Pohier, Schillebeeckx, Küng, the Jesuits, Sr Theresa Kane), then neutral observers may begin to feel that the 'Polish model' owes rather too much to the Communist Party to which it is so strongly opposed.

Many other examples could be given to confirm this point. The mass media are suspected of the worst and to be excluded from events such as the Dutch Synod (14-31 January 1980) and the autumn 1980 Synod on the Family. The univocal approach to ministry, conceived in Tridentine terms as a permanent state of life carrying with it status, and sharply differentiated from the more unpredictable and less controllable 'lay ministries', is another debt to the Polish inheritance. The refusal to take women seriously, while treating them with the utmost chivalry, is another 'Polish' trait. Above all, and as a synthesis of the preceding points, the Polish tradition has no experience, either in its own life or in the recent life of the nation, of democracy, and therefore it cannot comprehend the idea of 'loyal dissent'.

One thus reaches the conclusion that a particular model of the Church, evolved in a situation of oppression and admirably suited to those distressing circumstances, cannot easily be extended to the universal Church. The point was put most forcibly by Paul Thibaud writing in *Espirit* in April 1979. 'In Poland,' he wrote, 'the Catholic Church has the dual advantage of being both powerful and separate from power—simultaneously strong and innocent' (English translation in *Commonweal*, 14 September 1979). It is innocent because it does not have responsibility. It is powerful because it can articulate mass aspirations. But it follows that the move from opposition to leadership is fraught with difficulties.

Peter Steinfels

Neo-Conservatism in the United States

AMERICAN neo-conservatism is the last social-political outlook to emerge from the Sixties. It began as a reaction against the Sixties—but not a reaction of the right. For the most part, American neo-conservatives were men of the moderate left—'liberals', as the term is used in the US—and many of them would insist on being called liberals even today. Influential in the universities and Washington, these individuals felt confident by the mid-Sixties that their own views promised the United States a future of practical, efficient, orderly change. Instead the future turned out to be one of urban riots, racial conflict, bitter national division over the war in Vietnam, the excesses of the 'counter-culture', disruption of higher education, a Nixon presidency, and harsh criticism directed at these liberals themselves. The latter, understandably, felt betrayed. Neo-conservatism was their response.

1. FEAR OF CULTURAL CHAOS

Neo-conservatism in the US has never been a tightly formulated political doctrine. It is a current of opinion, a set of priorities, a selection of problems, a preference for certain types of explanations, a consensus about who the 'enemy' is. Neo-conservatism is also a largely negative, critical outlook, concerning its energies more on the elimination of what it considers errors than on making positive proposals. Thus one would be hard put to identify 'neo-conservative solutions' even to the major domestic problems facing the American Government: unemployment, inflation, energy. But one could easily identify those 'solutions' that would earn neo-conservative ire—for example, any significant extensions of government economic planning, jobs programmes, or income policies; likewise, anti-nuclear militancy and protective environmental regulation.

At the core of neo-conservatism is a fear of cultural chaos and a desire to establish cultural discipline. Neo-conservatives believe that the governing institutions of American society, and probably of the democratic nations generally, are caught in a crisis of confidence. Authority has been undermined, the legitimacy of institutions threatened. This conviction they share, of course, with many thinkers on the left. But unlike left-wing observers, neo-conservatives do not view this challenge to authority as truly 'earned' by any thorough-going failures of political leadership or of social or economic institutions. Nor do they join the left in seeing the crisis of legitimacy as deeply rooted in flawed social-political or economic structures. Instead they see the source of current difficulties as specifically and independently cultural. The dominant cultural outlook has been infected with a systematic hostility to authority—an infection which different neo-conservatives trace back variously to Romanticism, bohemianism, Marxism, and other nineteenth-century expressions of revolt against the bourgeois world-view. Today this 'adversary culture' manifests itself in the blatant hedonism of the counter-culture but perhaps more seductively in the more genteel quest for 'self-fulfilment' on the part of the educated and affluent. It equally manifests itself in the political nihilism of revolutionary terrorism—but also, in transmuted form, in the militant environmentalism or identification with Third World grievances, both of which appear to question the material and moral bases of western industrial societies.

2. THE NEW CLASS

When neo-conservatives are tempted to link this cultural deformation to changes in the social structure, they point to the extended reach of higher education, the government, and the media. The expansion of higher education was a response to the need of advanced industrial societies for theoretically trained and certified personnel— what the neo-conservatives term a 'new class'. If expanded higher education has exposed this massive new class to the adversarial mentality that was once the possession only of anti-bourgeois coteries, the expansion of government and the media has magnified the new class's influence.

The adversarial tendency of the new class is also magnified by social problems that do exist in the United States, primarily the problem of a large element within the poor and minorities—an 'underclass' it is frequently called—that has the characteristics of Marx's *lumpen-proletariat*, and whose condition can realistically (according to the neo-conservatives) be ameliorated only slowly, if at all. In the plight of the poor and minorities—a dramatic contradiction to the nation's traditional acclamation of equality—the new class has a powerful weapon for undermining the legitimacy of social institutions. But beneath the supposed altruism of this dedication to equality, the new class is ruthlessly pursuing its own self-interest—assuaging guilt over its own new-found affluence; expanding government power (and therefore its own opportunities for employment and influence) at the expense of the previously dominant business class and the heavily burdened lower middle-class taxpayers. The fact that the resulting political agitation places demands upon government that government is simply unable to meet only further saps public confidence and the legitimacy of institutions.

At this point one might well ask what divides American neo-conservatism from traditional conservatism. Three things. First, neo-conservatism is the adopted outlook of a cosmopolitan group of intellectuals, and social scientists in particular, whereas much American 'conservatism' including much of Mr Reagan's New Right constituency, represents the frustration of rural, small-town, and religiously fundamentalist citizens who have lost cultural and economic dominance. Though neo-conservatives and the New Right often express similar demands for cultural discipline, the former can argue from a thorough-going familiarity with modern thought; their conservatism has a greater claim to being called *post-modern* rather than pre-modern. Second, neo-conservatism does not, like some strands of traditional American conservatism, reject industrial society. It has no nostalgia for an agrarian past or the rugged individualism of the frontiersman and cowboy. Third, neo-conservatism, unlike the other major strand of American conservatism (which, in fact, is a transmutation of nineteenth-century *laissez-faire* liberalism), does not argue a root-and-branch rejection of the Welfare State. The litmus test for liberalism and conservatism in the US has long been Franklin Roosevelt's New Deal. Conservatives have considered it an aberration from American principles, a break in the proper continuity of national tradition. On this, the neo-conservatives stand with liberals. They approve of the New Deal and *in principle* of a moderate Welfare State. They offer, instead, pragmatic reasons for not extending the Welfare State further at this period of history.

In this sense, the extension of government services and powers associated with the New Deal holds a place in American political debate somewhat like the Second Vatican Council in the Catholic Church. The liberals and the left see this New Deal legacy largely as a starting point; in so far as it established a greater modicum of equality and social justice in the United States, equality and social justice require further social change. Neo-conservatives, while accepting the New Deal reforms as valuable, see a greater need to contain the spirit of further change and forestall innovations that might risk institutional instability. Traditional conservatives remain unreconciled to the New Deal almost in its entirety.

3. A CULTURAL STRATEGY

Given this analysis of the social situation, what did the neo-conservatives propose to do? They did what intellectuals always do: write articles, publish books, criticise other books, give free advice to whatever opinion-makers or political figures would listen. Starting about 1970 their public discussion adopted what one of their most influential editors called 'a new approach and a new tone'. To begin with, although the war in Vietnam was still raging and social and economic policy had reached a turning point, the neo-conservative intellectuals were convinced, as another of them declared, that 'our main task' was to attack the left—and not only to 'argue with it' but 'to strip it ultimately of the pretension that it understands the causes of our ills and how to set them right'. Stripping the left of its pretensions meant mounting a systematic offensive against almost every expression of liberal and radical reform. A barrage of articles began to appear in neo-conservative journals; not only were liberal and radical ideas subjected to sharp criticism, but as the same editor boasted, their advocates' 'motives were subjected to a skeptical "demystifying" scrutiny'.

A decade of frantic and often frustrating activity, plus the anarchic and anti-intellectual spirit of the counter-culture, had resulted in more than a little intellectual flabbiness on the left—and made it an easy target for neo-conservative criticism. The momentum of political and cultural radicalism had been broken by the first years of the decade in any case. Yet neo-conservatism did not curb its offensive. At least three developments spurred the neo-conservatives further to the right. The first was Watergate and the discrediting of the Nixon administration, which a number of neo-conservatives had taken the unpopular step (unpopular among intellectuals) of supporting publicly. The fact that this support had now become a source of embarrassment only seemed to lead the neo-conservatives to attack the left all the more vigorously, as if in self-justification. The second development was the shift in international power, as marked by American withdrawal from Vietnam, Egypt's strong showing in the '73 war with Israel, and the emergent economic leverage of OPEC. Although many neo-conservatives were not supporters of America's role in Vietnam, they were deeply committed to US containment of Soviet power and to the security of Israel. They turned, therefore, to international affairs, where they found the same crisis of authority and vacillating will as they had in domestic politics—and where they

D

prescribed the same remedy, a new national assertiveness by the United States. This, of course, produced whole new areas of contention with the liberals and the left.

The third development is more complex. Disturbed by Sixties' radicalism and the counter-culture's rejection of commercial and industrial values, assailed by environmental legislation, and aware of the inevitable importance of government in economic management, American business leaders have increasingly given greater attention to shaping a climate of public opinion favourable to their concerns. The neo-conservatives were not originally attached to business—they were independent intellectuals, university men, and civil servants. But they shared with business a common set of adversaries on the left and a concern with a more settled cultural mood. An alliance has formed. Large-scale advertising campaigns by major corporations mix neo-conservative criticism of the 'new class' with traditional business complaints about governmental interference. Business liberally funds research centres where neo-conservative scholars work in proximity with monetarist and *laissez-faire* economists. The end result is that neo-conservatives have become very solicitous of capitalism's reputation (some have even set to work constructing a new 'theology of democratic capitalism'); business has gained a new legitimacy in the intellectual world; and neo-conservative themes are given much wider currency in the government and media.

Nonetheless, this remarkable success has taken its toll. But in its assertive foreign policy and its defence of corporate capitalism, neo-conservatism has lost much of its distinctiveness from traditional conservatism. Its ultimate answer to the problem of cultural anarchy is the construction of a *clerisy*, a caste of intellectuals whose vocation is primarily to erect a barricade of scepticism between new ideas and the arena of 'responsible' public discussion. The neo-conservative concern with cultural coherence and discipline is not unreasonable. But neo-conservatives act as though the dissolvents of that coherence and discipline are infections from 'outside' the established social structures rather than rooted within them. In sealing a pact with capitalism against any threatening social, cultural, or economic innovation, the neo-conservatives may be blocking the possibility of discovering the very coherence they seek.

Gregory Baum

Neo-Conservative Critics
of the Churches

THIS IS a preliminary essay on a topic that has not been carefully researched. In recent years Christian individuals and groups have reacted very strongly against 'the shift to the left' that has taken place in the social teaching of the Christian Churches and Church Councils. In North America in particular, Christians who sometimes call themselves 'neo-conservatives' have raised theological difficulties, proposed new political ideals and recommended new pastoral policies to the churches.[1]

1. THE NEW SOCIAL GOSPEL

What is meant by 'the shift to the left' in ecclesiastical teaching? In the social doctrine formulated by the highest authorities of Church bodies, Anglican, Protestant and Catholic, as well as by Church Councils, we find an essentially identical analysis of the structures of sin characteristic of today's society. We are told that something is wrong with contemporary capitalism. Capitalism widens the gap between the rich and the poor, especially between rich and poor nations; it permits the power over resources and production to pass into the hands of an ever smaller élite; it not only produces exploitation in many parts of the world, including regions of poverty in the industrialised countries, but it also creates a materialistic culture, an achievement- and pleasure-oriented business civilisation that estranges people from the substance of their humanity. What these Church documents advocate is a more rationally planned economy, greater sharing of wealth and more participation in decision-making, the extension of democratic processes to economic life, and the examination of local and national problems in the light of the needs of the entire global community.

The Catholic Church in North America has followed this new approach. By way of illustration I wish to refer to two ecclesiastical documents. The first is the Labour Day Statement of 1976, written by the Canadian Catholic bishops, entitled 'From Words to Action', which focuses on the injustices in Canadian society, defines social sin in terms of institutional oppression, and outlines various steps in the struggle for justice in Canada. These steps include the re-reading of the Scriptures from the viewpoint of the poor, a willingness to listen to the marginalised and disadvantaged people and peoples of Canada, a careful analysis of the socio-economic causes of injustice and oppression, and political action to remove these causes from society. The bishops acknowledge that this new discipleship of Jesus has been embraced only by a small minority of Catholics, but they call it 'a significant minority' because it summons the entire Church to greater fidelity.

The second document I wish to mention is the pastoral letter, 'This Land is Home to Me', signed by twenty-five American bishops of the region of Appalachia, a poor region of the United States. The pastoral letter analyses what social sin means in that part of the country and what steps should be taken leading towards social salvation. The structural evil that has led to perpetual exploitation of the Appalachians is an economic system characterised by two principles, 'technological rationality' and 'maximisation of profit'. Technological rationality assures that the decisions regarding the land and its people are made in terms of perfecting the technological functioning of the extractive industries and the production connected with them. Decisions affecting people's lives are here made as if workers were tools in the process of production. The maximisation of profit, the essential principle of capitalism in its early and in later phases, assures that decisions regarding production aim at increasing the profit of owners or investors and hence at drawing from the workers the maximum labour power at the lowest price that is legally possible. Both of these principles, the Catholic bishops tell us, are at odds with the Church's social teaching. As remedy the pastoral letter advocates the co-operation of various centres of power in the country such as federal and state governments, labour unions and citizens' organisations, in restricting the power of the large corporations and forcing them to make decisions in consultation with the Appalachians concerned with protecting their land and its inhabitants.

We note in passing that these two documents, as well as other ecclesiastical statements on social justice, have adopted elements of liberation theology without being wholly committed to its theoretical basis. In particular, ecclesiastical teaching accepts the notion of social sin, recognises that the redemption which Jesus brought includes the liberation of people from the structures of oppression, and affirms that the demand for social justice is an essential element of the Christian message. These ecclesiastical documents do not go as far as liberation theology in as much as they do not analyse to what extent the Church itself as part of the dominant culture has become a symbol of legitimation for the conditions of oppression. The ecclesiastical documents, therefore, do not try to formulate Christian message and Christian prayer in a more politically responsible manner.

2. THE OLD SOCIAL GOSPEL

Some of the neo-conservative critics of the Churches have argued that the new Social Gospel is simply a revival of the discredited old Social Gospel, which had its beginnings in the last decades of the nineteenth century, reached a high point in the years prior to World War I, and continued, albeit in weakened form, into the Twenties. These critics believe that Reinhold Niebuhr's refutation of the Social Gospel in the Thirties and early Forties retains its validity in regard to the present movement. Niebuhr criticises the Social Gospel for two reasons.[2] First, he argued that the advocates of the Social Gospel were liberals, inspired by ideas of social evolution, insensitive to the reality of sin and ignorant of the vast power held by the classes that defend the existing order. Whether this criticism is valid for the best theologians of the Social Gospel is questionable: Niebuhr's arguments aimed more directly at a certain widely-spread mood, moralistic and optimistic, created by the Social Gospel. Niebuhr formulated his criticism in the Thirties when he himself was strongly influenced by Marxist thought. Marx's sense of class struggle and what Niebuhr called 'his catastrophism' appealed to the American theologian who then understood the biblical doctrine of sin as the conclusive repudiation of social evolution and trust in progressivism. Secondly, Niebuhr opposed the Social Gospel because it seemed to him that its social policies were based on unrealistic expectations in regard to the future, on what he called a 'Utopian' vision of history, and on a false interpretation of the divine promises. God's promises, Niebuhr argued, cannot be fulfilled in history. To expect the coming of the kingdom in historical time is not only an expression of naïvete, it represents even more a loss of the sense of divine transcendence.

Do these arguments retain their validity *vis-à-vis* the new Social Gospel of contemporary Church documents and liberation theology? They do not. In the first place, the new Social Gospel is critical of liberalism, overwhelmed by a sense of social evil, keenly aware of the powers that oppose justice and peace, and is in fact strongly affected by Marxist thought, the social theory that influenced Niebuhr to reject the old Social Gospel. In the second place, neither Church documents nor liberation theology expect the coming of God's kingdom into history. The theological rationale of the Christian political commitment is not taken principally from eschatology. Contemporary theologians have learnt from the mistakes of the old Social Gospel. The Utopia for tomorrow is clearly distinguished from the kingdom of God ever pressing upon us and yet ever unrealised. The theological reason for the Christian commitment to social justice is what is sometimes called 'the option for the poor'. This means that when confronted by social struggles and the conflict of power, the Christian, following the call of Jesus Christ, opts for solidarity with 'the poor', the oppressed, the marginalised, the peoples and classes that suffer dehumanisation by existing social, economic and political structures. It is not a naïve expectation of God's kingdom that makes Christians critics of contemporary capitalism; it is rather faith in Jesus Christ as the one who judges the structures of sin, who reveals that the human world can be changed, whose grace empowers people to act, and whose message is a vector moving history toward the overcoming of dehumanising social systems.

We note that in this new Social Gospel we have the identification of social radicalism and religious orthodoxy. The transcendent Trinitarian mystery of God is seen as present in history and operative in the lives of men and women and their societies. This theory is sometimes called 'panentheism'. Here the infinite does not stand over and against the finite; here the infinite is in and through the finite—as matrix, as judgment, as summons, as power, as creativity, as horizon. According to Christian dogma this theory is in keeping with orthodoxy as long as the union of the infinite and the finite is seen not as a product of necessity or natural law, but as based on grace, on divine initiative, on personal gift, on God's free self-communication.

3. THEOLOGICAL OBJECTIONS

The attack on the new Social Gospel (usually formulated by social thinkers who are not theologians) often presents itself as a defence of divine transcendence, although not in the Niebuhrian sense of that word. Because the new Social Gospel understands the Christian message as revealing the divine involvement in the transformation of the world, it is accused of overlooking divine transcendence. What the accusations mean by divine transcendence, however, is the reference to a superior divine world, elevated above human history, towards which Christians are destined by their faith and/or the existence of the sacred radically distinct from the profane, the *tremendum et fascinosum*, the divine self-manifestation in historical moments of worship and ecstacy. The neo-conservative 'Hartford Theses', originally planned by Richard Neuhaus and Peter Berger, were intended to be a public warning against trends in modern Church life that overlook divine transcendence.[3] What was being criticised was the view that Christian revelation is the entry of God into man's making of man, into the redemption of history, into the process of humanisation, emancipation and pacification of the entire human race. In the perspective of the Hartford Theses, such an understanding of Christian revelation is too 'secular' and too this-worldly: it tends to weaken people's sense of the supernatural, make them neglect the heavenly world in their hearts and engender indifference to their own death and the life that awaits beyond it.

Yet the neo-conservative defenders of 'transcendence' have failed to offer appropriate theological arguments. For them the 'transcendent' is honoured either by acknowledging a heavenly world or by accepting the division of life into the sacred and the profane. For reasons of their own, they want to defend this perception of transcendence at all costs. But in the Scriptures the most extraordinary manifestation of divine reality is in the human passage from sin to grace, in the Spirit-created conversion of the heart, in the Passover from oppression to freedom and from death to life. To believe in a divinity in heaven is not Christian faith unless that divinity be seen as gracious towards men and women, redemptively involved in their lives, and present to them as a source of new life: and to experience the *tremendum et fascinosum* is not Christian unless it initiates the worshippers to personal transformation and empowers them to responsible action in the world. Neither the affirmation of a heavenly world nor the encounter of the sacred implies divine transcendence in properly Christian terms. The encounter with God in faith is always redemptive. Ecstasies and elevations are not moments of transcendence in the Christian sense if they do not transform the worshippers as they return to earth and face their fellow human beings. Classical Christianity, in its traditional dualistic and its modern panentheistic form, acknowledges that God's self-revelation and self-communication is salvational, *propter nostram salutem*, aimed at the transformation of human life.

In *Christianity and the World Order*, an attack on the new Social Gospel, the English historian Edward Norman argues that the social teaching the Churches have adopted over the last decade, undermines Christian faith because it does not express man's relationship to eternity and because it does not reflect religious experience. Let us look at these arguments separately. Norman claims that the Christian message is 'by nature concerned primarily with the relationship of the soul to eternity'. This pietistic interpretation of Christianity can hardly claim the support of the New Testament and the ancient creeds. Jesus has always been understood as the saviour of the world. God has always been proclaimed as creator, redeemer and sanctifier of humankind. The advent of Christ was clearly recognised as an event of world historical meaning and consequence. It is true, of course, that this world historical dimension was not usually understood in terms of socio-political transformation: such a reading of the gospel had to wait for the emergence of a critical political imagination in western history. But at no time in the Church's history has the redemption brought by Jesus Christ been summed up as access of human souls to eternity. Even from the beginning, the Church saw itself as God's people with a mission and destiny in history.

How is the new Social Gospel related to religious experience? When we read the literature produced by writers identified with political or liberation theology we learn that the inherited piety has indeed become problematic. The religious experience into which Christians were initiated usually encouraged a dualistic perception of Christian faith. Piety often reflected an understanding of the God/man relationship that today no longer fits the socio-critical stance adopted by many Christians, especially in Third World churches. In the light of the new Social Gospel, the self-enclosed soul or self has become problematic. Is a person's isolated existence *vis-à-vis* the rest of society and *vis-à-vis* God divinely planned? Or does it rather express an alienated state, induced by a competitive economic system and an individualistic spiritual culture? I wish to argue that the Church's new social teaching is based on, and accompanied by new religious experiences, at odds with pietism, which explode the walls of self, reveal to people that they are embedded in classes or movements and generate a new sense of solidarity with others. This transcendence of soul-centredness is experienced as divinely grounded, as a gift, as something to be grateful for, as God's presence. The only way a person lives authentically is to let 'the others' become part of his or her own self-destination.

Some Latin American Christian poets have been overwhelmed by the liberationist perspective implicit in their religious experiences. Their encounters with divinity do not elevate them above history and detach them from the miseries of this world. Such experience would be regarded as politically dangerous by them. Religious experience for them is a gracious entry into a consciousness that discerns God not as the invisible other whose presence dims the world, as the Alone with the alone, but on the contrary as ground, vector and horizon that unite them with their brothers and sisters struggling for justice. Religious experience here makes people recognise, with fear, trembling and ecstasy, the place assigned to them in salvation history. God is the link to others, solidarity, the forward movement uniting those who yearn for redemption.

For many Christians committed to social justice, religious language has become suspect because the meaning assigned to this language by the dominant culture legitimates the existing order despite its injustices. For this reason these Christians often refuse to speak about inwardness and religious experience. They search for a secular vocabulary. Sometimes they create the impression that they have little interest in the openness of faith to the divine voice and the divine presence. Catholic activists, I am prepared to argue, do not see a conflict between political radicalism and the mystical tradition. The ancient Catholic teaching of the *via negativa*, the dialectical negation of all God-language, has a special affinity to the new spiritual direction of the contemporary Social Gospel.

4. THE NEW CLASS

The neo-conservative authors, we repeat, do not only oppose liberation theology and political theology; they also criticise the social teaching of the churches which, as we have seen, has been influenced by liberation theology but does not follow its method in a consistent manner. The neo-conservative authors believe that the churches have been seduced into error. Peter Berger argues that the churches lost their nerve in the Sixties when they permitted themselves to be influenced by youth culture and protest movements and integrated some of their aspirations into the Christian understanding of freedom.[4] The neo-conservative writers suggest that the churches and Church Councils have been misguided by radical men and women on their staff. Edward Norman makes explicit use of a neo-conservative theory to explain the Church's shift to the left. He argues that the ecclesiastical staff workers responsible for the new policies belong to the so-called 'new class', the group of intellectual and cultural agents that produce science and the works of culture and that, for reasons of their own, have made Marxism the fashionable philosophy.

The theory of the new class is used by the neo-conservative thinkers to explain the widespread unrest and discontent in the relatively affluent countries of the West. Why are the young people so unhappy? Why do the various minorities lose their patience? Why do women aspire to new power in society? Why do people criticise the capitalist system that has enriched them? The reason for this unrest, we are told, is not found in the contradictions and injustices built into the institutions of modern society, which inflict alienation and oppression upon various sections of the population; the reason is rather to be found in the influence of the growing class of disgruntled intellectual and social workers who spread discontent and criticism through their cultural creativity. We notice that while neo-conservatives are usually 'liberals' in their political philosophy, here they adopt a classical conservative theory, first elaborated by Edmund Burke, who assigned the cause of the French Revolution not to the oppression of the *ancien régime* but to the destructive influence of French philosophers and political thinkers. Contemporary neo-conservatives offer several reasons why today's intellectuals spread contempt for capitalist society.

The members of the new class are usually employed by government in schools and other agencies. They are envious of scientists and engineers who work for private enterprise and receive higher remuneration. The new class is envious of the salaries paid by industry. The intellectuals despise business skills and entrepreneurship. The men and women of the new class have become hyper-critical of society because they do not have access to power. For this reason they concentrate on the negative aspects of present society, they belittle the achievements of the present system and overlook the manner in which they themselves have profited from it. They focus on the inequalities in capitalist society, some of which are simply connatural to any social order. Through their writings they make people impatient with their lot and engender in them wholly unrealistic expectations in regard to the future. What the new class wants is more power. They involve themselves with minorities and offer their help to the underprivileged because this disguises their own selfish aims and grants them a moral victory over the rest of society. They want to gain power with the backing of these minorities. The new class favours the public over the private sector, and for this reason has become critical of capitalism. The extension of government spending on education, social service and poverty programmes creates jobs for members of their own class. They promote a social theory that protects their own economic interests. And they turn to Marxism as the intellectual weapon against the present system because it suits their anger. Today Marxist theory in the capitalist countries has become an ideology of the new class in its quest for greater social power. The neo-conservative critics of the churches argue that members of this new class have gained influence in ecclesiastical agencies and are responsible for the churches' shift to the left.

This theory of the new class is unconvincing. It is in fact outrageous to suggest that people protest against economic exploitation, racial discrimination and other forms of inferiorisation only because they have become victims of subversive propaganda.

Still, the question does remain why the churches at this time have opted for a left-wing perspective. What are the social forces that have moved ecclesiastical organisations to this new approach? The great majority of Christians has certainly remained indifferent to the question of social justice. The Canadian bishops, in their pastoral declaration, openly admitted that only a minority of Catholics follow the new approach. They added that this minority is often under attack in the congregations, especially 'by the more affluent and powerful sector' of the Catholic community. It would not be difficult to demonstrate that the shift to the left in the churches' teaching is to a large extent due to the impact of Third World Christians on the consciousness of First World churches. This process began at the Geneva Conference of Church and Society in 1966. For the Roman Catholic Church, the significant turning point was the Synod of Bishops held at Rome in 1971 where the Latin American perspective worked out at the Medellín Conference (1968) was taken up in the social teaching of the world episcopate. At the level of the highest leadership the churches have recognised that the basic conflict in present society is between North and South, between the industrialised countries of the capitalist West and the socialist East on the one hand and on the other the underdeveloped countries of the other continents that are moving into greater dependency, destitution, and related forms of human misery. It is here, in the encounter with the Third World, that the Christian churches have discovered that the issue of private ownership of resources and productive machinery has become a moral and even a spiritual problem.

While we reject the theory of the new class in the form outlined above, it is possible to argue that salaried persons with a modest income, whose work is interesting and demands dedication, such as Church workers, social workers, teachers and other persons employed in cultural tasks, often display great sympathy for a socialist system in which all work in society is remunerated on precisely these terms. Why could not everyone work and live that way? These people realise that the wealthy would find it difficult to lower their standard of living, but they often forget that the great majority of workers have such burdensome and uninteresting jobs that dedication is not an adequate recompense. Moreover, to people who work for the Church organisations and pastoral programmes simplicity or 'the simple life' has a special spiritual meaning, and hence they easily think that their own life style is an answer to the grave problems of the present.

5. DEFENCE OF CAPITALISM AND PASTORAL POLICY

The neo-conservative critics consider it their special responsibility to defend the present capitalist system. Michael Novak has made this the major effort of his intellectual career.[5] Capitalism is the indispensable basis of social pluralism and personal freedom. In particular, the critics offer an alternative theory of contemporary alienation, one which accounts for the malaise of modernity in terms of the growing influence of technology and bureaucratic administration. Following Max Weber they argue that technocratic society with mega-structures dominating every sphere of human life, is gradually undermining personal freedom and personal creativity. Modern society, moreover, defined by increasing rationalisation, dissolves traditional values, secularises social bonds and religious symbols, and destroys the non-rational aspects of life that give meaning and joy to human living. The neo-conservative critics use this theory to show that the socialist analysis of alienation is wrong. It is not the division of society into rich and poor, masters and servants, owners and workers, that is the principal cause of present unhappiness; it is rather the growing rationalisation of life that causes dehumanisation and affects people in the wealthy suburbs as well as the poor neighbourhoods. Alienation transcends class division. The view that socialism would significantly transform human life is an illusion, a dangerous myth, which makes people dream of an impossible future, sends them into Utopian politics that are bound to fail, and weakens their will to reform present society.

The neo-conservative writers even criticise the shift to the left in the Church's social teaching, even though this teaching does not go as far as recommending a socialist economy. The reason why capitalist society is so chaotic at this time, neo-conservatives argue, is that people are no longer dedicated to it. What has taken place is a crisis of culture. People have become soft; they shy away from hard work; they seek personal fulfilment and pleasure; they have abandoned what Max Weber called 'the Protestant ethic'. Contemporary permissive culture, we are repeatedly told, is at odds with requirements of the economic system. Neo-conservative writers ask the churches to return to a more authoritarian form of religion and make normative again the old virtues of industry, dedication, sacrifice and asceticism. In today's world the Christian religion must become the guardian of public virtues and the symbol system that promotes consensus in society. Religion must live up to its essential nature of being the sacred canopy sheltering the social order. (We notice here the inner connection between the neo-conservatives' stress on transcendence and their defence of the present order.)

In the writings of Peter Berger, the neo-conservative position is elaborated with great sophistication.[6] Berger is more sensitive to the malaise of modernity than other neo-conservatives, but he agrees with them that in the developed countries of the West socialism offers a wholly illusory solution. Capitalism is here to stay. Even the mega-structures that dominate all aspects of public life and induce a sense of impotence and meaninglessness, cannot be overcome: they are demanded by the giant proportions industrialisation has achieved. What men and women have to learn is to survive in capitalist society and save their humanity. What is needed in this predicament is the creation of 'mediating structures', small organisations in which members still know one another, make joint decisions and mediate life to one another in a personal way. Mediating structures can be religious congregations, ethnic organisations, urban neighbourhoods and other voluntary associations. We must create islands of authentic humanity in the midst of the technocratic society that supplies us with material goods but leads to spiritual despair. The important pastoral task of the churches, therefore, is the creation of tightly woven parishes and communities, in which people can experience themselves as creative human beings. Local churches must become oases of human happiness. Berger suggests that the churches should drop their critical approach to capitalism and the promotion of radical social change: they should turn to a wholly different pastoral task, the formation of mediating structures, in which people can find God and their humanity.

Berger's emphasis on mediating structures is important. Emile Durkheim was the first sociologist who recognised the need for such institutions in modern society. Yet from a Christian point of view it is important to distinguish between mediating structures that isolate people in their own circle of contentment and those that bring people together in supportive communities, strengthening them to assume social responsibility for the wider society. The first kind, the islands of happiness, detach people from the societal project and hence strengthen the existing order, while the second kind, the supportive communities with wider outreach, are dynamic agents of social change. If the churches want to learn from the sociology of mediating structures and at the same time remain faithful to their social teaching, they should conceive their parishes and congregations as missionary communities, as communities where vital, personal interchange nourishes authentic humanity and at the same time generates urgent concern for justice in society.

How strong will this neo-conservative trend become in the churches? On the highest level of authority at least, the churches will remain committed to a spirituality that includes concern for the hungry sector of humankind and thus continues to promote radical social criticism.

Notes

1. The best known authors in the USA are Peter Berger, Richard Neuhaus and Michael Novak. Their views are endorsed by other writers and editors of Church publications. In England Edward Norman has begun to write in the same vein.

2. See the articles by John Bennett and Arthur Schlesinger in *Reinhold Niebuhr: His Religious, Social and Political Thought*, edited by C. W. Kegley and R. W. Bretall (New York 1961).

3. The so-called Hartford Appeal denounced thirteen erroneous theses that allegedly pervaded American theology. See *Against the World for the World*, ed. P. Berger and R. Neuhaus (New York 1976).

4. P. Berger *Facing Up to Modernity* (New York 1977) p. 194.

5. See J. L. Walsh 'Making the Case for Capitalism' *Commonweal* (22 June 1979) 366-369.

6. See P. Berger *The Homeless Mind* (New York 1974).

Pablo Richard

Progressive Neo-Conservatism in Latin America

INTRODUCTION

THE BASIC contrast in the Church in Latin America is between the *ruling Christendom* and the *Church that springs from the people*. Progressive neo-conservatism is the political and theological current that seeks to re-construct Christendom, as opposed to the movement of liberating evengelisation, which is renewing and converting the Church under the guidance of the Holy Spirit.

This article sets out to analyse the origin, development and viewpoint of this progressive neo-conservatism. This is a new current, springing from classical conservatism and social Christianity, so we need to look at these, their social and ecclesial content and the model of Christendom they embody. Then we need to study the crisis in which both find themselves, with reference to the aspects of this crisis specific to Latin America. Progressive neo-conservatism offers itself as an alternative as a result of this crisis, seeking to re-structure the classic model of Christendom.

The general framework for this article is the contemporary history of the Church in Latin America. Analysis of progressive neo-conservatism is always seen against the liberating movement for renewal in the Church. So we are studying a negative phenomenon within a generally positive framework.

1. CLASSIC CONSERVATISM

This is basically defined by the *unconditional legitimisation* which the Church gives to any ruling structure or power. Historically, this type of conservatism has had two forms of expression. The first, traditional-religious, always accepts whatever power or authority happens to be ruling or established as legitimate. The basis of this attitude is found in a literal interpretation of Romans 13:1: 'Let every person be subject to the governing authorities. For there is no authority except from God, and those that exist have been instituted by God.' So authority is legitimate simply because it exists, because it rules, because it is constituted. The second, modern-ideological, consists in the Church underwriting the legitimacy of the ruling powers by explicitly taking on the ideology or political theory on which this power is based. An example of this would be that minority of bishops in Latin America who support military dictatorships by

51

explicitly backing the doctrine of National Security. In sociological terms, we would say that the Church, in modern conservatism, integrates itself into civil society by legitimising the ethical and theoretical bases of political society.

2. SOCIAL CHRISTIANITY

This current arose as a progressive alternative, in opposition to conservatism. Since the Sixties, most of the bishops have moved from conservatism to social Christianity, which can be defined by the *conditional legitimacy* the Church grants to the ruling structure or powers. The legitimacy of an authority is subordinated to a series of conditions laid down by the Church. So both conservatism and social Christianity share a legitimisation of the established powers, but with the first this is unconditional and absolute, while with the second it is conditional and relative.

Social Christianity has also taken on different historical forms in Latin America, according to the type of conditioning to which legitimisation of the ruling powers has been made subject. One form is doctrinal in character, where the conditions are reduced to an abstract, formal statement of the social teaching of the Church. Another is humanist in character, where the Church is not content with a general statement of principles, but makes legitimacy conditional on a series of specific and verifiable requirements, such as respect for human rights, a programme for overcoming particular forms of extreme poverty, illiteracy, infant mortality, etc. Another expression of social Christianity is political, when the Church judges the legitimacy of a system or authority not only on the basis of particular situations of poverty or injustice, but on that of a certain political programme or theory. In countries with military régimes, for example, the Church might make acceptance of the legitimacy of the régime conditional on restoration of a State based on the rule of law, or a political programme for the re-establishment of democracy.

3. SOCIO-ECCLESIAL PRACTICE AND MODELS OF THE CHURCH

Conservatism and social Christianity are not only theories, doctrines or ideologies, but always embody both social and ecclesial practice. These practices, in turn, define different types or models of the Church, in which the social role or function of the Church will vary from case to case. But in both conservatism and social Christianity, the dominant model of the Church is that of *Christendom*. Christendom is defined as a specific form of insertion of the Church in the overall social fabric, through the mediation of the ruling social and political powers. The degree of this mediation will vary according to the degree of legitimacy the Church accords to the ruling powers. Conservatism presents a model of Christendom in which integration of the hierarchical Church into the political structure converts it into an ideological apparatus of the State. This integration is greatest in the case of modern conservatism.

In social Christianity, the model of the Church is still that of Christendom, but the degree of integration of the Church with the political structure is less. The more the hierarchical Church conditions the legitimacy of the ruling powers, the greater its freeedom *vis-à-vis* those powers. The hierarchical Church practising social Christianity of the humanist type will generally exercise a mediatory role in regard to the State, interceding for all those who are persecuted or repressed. When its social Christianity is political, then the hierarchy will have a para-party role in relation to the State, and identify itself with the democratic opposition to totalitarian régimes.

Both conservatism and social Christianity, in their socio-ecclesial practice, uphold the invariable basic structure of the model of Christendom. This basic structure is the relationship of legitimacy established between the Church and the State. As long as the model of Christendom is adhered to, both conservatism and social Christianity, whatever their form of expression (traditional, modern, doctrinal, humanist, political) will always be a source of legitimacy for the ruling political system.

Today, a new model of the Church is arising in Latin America. This breaks completely with the model of Christendom, whether its expression is conservative of social-Christian. It is a Church springing up on the margins of and against Christendom, offering no kind of legitimisation to the ruling powers or political system. This model of the Church is known as 'the people's Church' or 'the Church that springs from the people', and its existence was officially recognised in the Puebla Document (no. 263). This new model of the Church is not opposed to the hierarchical or official Church, but only to the model of Christendom. It is a Church that does not use the ruling political powers as a means of taking shape in society, but depends solely on the power of the gospel and the strength of its faith, hope and charity.

4. THE CRISIS OF CONSERVATISM AND SOCIAL CHRISTIANITY

One of the most important aspects of the present crisis of the capitalist system, in its under-developed and dependent form, is the *crisis of its legitimacy*. Today the masses of the Latin American population are everywhere becoming conscious of the illegitimacy of the ruling system. If conservatism is defined basically by the *unconditional legitimacy* it accords to the system, and social Christianity by the *conditional legitimacy* it accords, then obviously a *crisis of legitimacy* of the ruling capitalist system will have direct consequences for the constitutive basis of both conservatism and social Christianity. This crisis of legitimacy, which is fairly universal, has become unprecedentedly radical and widespread in Latin America during the Sixties and Seventies. During the same period, the crisis of legitimacy of the system has also caused a crisis in the socio-ecclesial practice and the model of Christendom employed by both conservative and social Christians, of equally radical nature and massive dimensions. If the ruling system has had its crises of legitimacy on other continents and at other times, why has this crisis in Latin America today become so radical and involved the Church so deeply? The answer to this question should lead to a better understanding of 'progressive neo-conservatism', which claims to be an alternative response to the present crisis of Christendom.

Three aspects of the crisis of legitimacy in Latin America

There are three aspects of processes specific to Latin America at this time, which answer the question.

(i) *The first process* is the specific form taken by the crisis of legitimacy of the system in Latin America. This crisis is perceived not as a purely technical problem, nor as a theoretical or political-ideological problem, but as a real problem on a massive scale, where what is at stake is nothing less than the *life or death* of vast sectors of the people of Latin America. Rather than because of any technical or ideological considerations, the system is everywhere seen to be illegitimate on account of its failure to assure the *life* of the majority of the people. These people are at present in real and permanent danger of collective *death*, in the sense that they have no means of finding work, food, shelter, health or education. Such a statement is not intellectual terrorism: the World Bank itself recognises that there are today 900 million people, mostly in the Third World, living in a state of abject poverty, and that in 1978 alone 30 million children under the age of five died of starvation.

As it has no future solution to this state of affairs, the system seeks to create an ideology or culture in which humanity can support or live with this problem in good conscience, accepting that the chances of survival for two-thirds of the world's population, most of them in the Third World, are marginal at best. In talking about the crisis of legitimacy of the system, I am not implying that it was legitimate before. It never was. The crisis only means that the impoverished masses are now becoming conscious on a massive scale of the illegitimacy of the ruling system, because of its failure to assure their *life*.

(ii) *The second process* is the way in which the 'traditional Christian' consciousness of Latin America has responded to the crisis of legitimacy of the capitalist system. Christianity, despite its age-long adulterations and manipulations, has always kept the evangelical sense of life alive. Faith in the resurrection and hope in the kingdom have been the ferment or evangelical nucleus which the poor have never forgotten or betrayed, despite all attempts at ideological domination by the ruling groups. In Latin America too, despite some 500 years of 'Christian' colonial rule, the poor have kept their ability to discern, assimilate and interiorise this subversive nucleus of evangelisation bearing on life. This deeply evangelical sense of life, which remains present in the exploited and believing people of Latin America, has enabled them to react to the *mortal* danger presented by a system which is incapable of assuring the *life* of the majority. Without this 'traditional Christian' sense of the people of Latin America, the crisis of legitimacy of the system, on the one hand, would not have had this widespread, conscious, deep realisation nor, on the other, would it have affected the whole of institutional Latin American Church so directly and deeply.

(iii) *The third process* which builds on and radicalises the two previous ones, is the social, political, ecclesial, theological and spiritual practice initiated by significant groups of Christians in Latin America from the Sixties to the present. These Christians, by living, expressing, communicating and celebrating their faith and hope in ecclesial form within the political struggle for the liberation of the poor and oppressed, have been able to generate a growing process of liberating evangelisation and theological, spiritual and ecclesial creativity. This process has deepened the final crisis of conservative and social-Christian *Christendom* and fortified the rise of 'a Church born of the people by the power of the Spirit of Christ'. This 'people's Church' has not arisen as an alternative to the hierarchical Church, but as an alternative to Christendom and a universal call to the only Church of Jesus. Though this third process is rooted in the two others, without it they would not have had so much effect on the central experience of the institutional churches.

5. LATIN AMERICAN 'PROGRESSIVE NEO-CONSERVATISM'

The final, irreversible crisis of conservative and social-Christian Christendom, and the rise of an ecclesial alternative on the fringe of and against this Christendom, has lately produced Latin American progressive neo-conservatism. This tendency seeks to rebuild Christendom with a new spirit, with new, progressive concerns and values. It does not question the basic structure of Christendom, but tries to give it new content and a new social role, so as to renew thereby the ecclesial life of the institutional Church. This progressive movement within Christendom is not afraid to integrate the concerns of the 'people's Church'—the crisis of the system, structural analysis of the socio-political reality, the problem of extreme poverty, popular religion, evangelisation, liberation, human rights, justice, solidarity, fraternity and the like—within its own social structures. But the fact that progressive neo-conservatism regards the basic structure of Christendom—legitimisation of the ruling political and social system as indispensable for assuring the presence and influence of the Church in society as a whole—as beyond question, determines its whole methodology.

Its integration of new, progressive concerns and values must therefore follow one of two courses. The first, proper to the conservatism that accords *unconditional* legitimisation to the ruling system, seeks to *rebuild the legitimacy* of the system now in crisis, by interpreting social reality on the basis of its new, progressive concerns and values, finding a new meaning in it and so being able to go on legitimising it. The second course, proper to social-Christian movements according *conditional* legitimacy to the system, seeks to *rebuild those conditions*. If it can integrate new concerns and progressive values, social Christianity can then maintain its legitimisation of the ruling system, which will then be subject to conditions whose meaning can be understood and supported by broader social strata, including those most anxious about the crisis of the system, and even by some of the poor people. In this way the social teaching of the Church, Christian humanism and the new political projects and programmes can be re-formulated, with their meaning adapted to the new, progressive concerns and values.

It is important not to criticise progressive neo-conservatism for the wrong reasons. The new concerns it embodies are good in themselves, its new values genuine, and both still fully valid. Nor is it guilty of bad faith or of a desire to dissimulate or distort reality as it sees it. Underlying conservatism, social Christianity and neo-conservatism, there is always the honest intent to evangelise and to build up the Church. Nor is neo-conservatism a strategy to win back the lost masses, or a diversionary tactic to confuse focus on basic problems. To judge it in this way would be erroneous, superficial and Manichean. This is not the basic problem.

The structural problem of conservatism in all its old and new manifestations, lies in the social and ecclesial practice which supports it and in the model of Christendom which gives it substance. The essence of this model of Christendom is the *legitimacy of the ruling powers*, whether this legitimacy is accorded conditionally or unconditionally. By this process of legitimisation, Christianity suffers a process of political reduction which converts it into an instrument of the ruling powers. In this form, it ceases to be a Christianity of faith, hope and charity, and becomes a Christianity of power and law. In order to evangelise, Christendom depends on the ruling social and political powers and is thereby reduced to the rule of law. The Church, on the other hand, evangelises by the power of its faith, hope and charity alone. Christendom, as here defined, transforms the Church seeking salvation through faith into a Church seeking salvation through law and power. Christendom implies a loss of faith and hope.

One can say of Christendom and of conservatism what St Paul said of the unjustified man, subject to the régime of law: 'I do not understand my own actions. For I do not do what I want but I do the very thing I hate' (Rom. 7:15; and see 7:7-25). In Christendom there is a gulf between intention and action, between purpose and practice, between content and achievement. It lacks both the capacity to express what it really does and that to bring about what it professes. Conservatism fails to carry out what it intends and does what it seeks to avoid. Its intention is good, its message and teaching orthodox, but it is incapable of saving and liberating mankind and society from the sin of the world. So it is under the rule of the law.

In Latin America, unfortunately, some highly-placed ecclesiastical institutions and persons, such as CELAM and some of its eminent theologians, have opted for the practice of the Christendom of progressive neo-conservatism. Not against them, but against this Christendom, the hope of a Church of faith is springing up, born of the People's Communities under the impulse of the Spirit of the Risen Christ.

Translated by Paul Burns

Michael Fleet

Neo-Conservatism in
Latin America

IN A world dominated by increasingly centralised economic and communications structures, ideas or social movements originating at the centre are unlikely to remain localised phenomena. Such is the case with the current upsurge of neo-conservatism, which has surfaced in countries of very different traditions and levels of development. In what follows, we describe neo-conservative trends in Latin America, the inroads they have made within the Catholic Church, and the factors that appear to preclude them from enjoying as full a flowering or wide an appeal as elsewhere.

1. LATIN AMERICA

At the heart of neo-conservatism is the inclination to 'leave well enough alone'. Neo-conservatives are erstwhile progressives now sceptical of efforts to create a new or just society. Some wistfully, others not, they have concluded that government attempts to eliminate poverty or inequality create more problems than they solve. Accordingly, they expect relatively little from government or politics, are more appreciative (and tolerant) of the existing order and its limitations, and seek personal fulfilment or consolation through private pursuits and associations.

In Latin America, such sentiments have gained ground in the last fifteen years. During this period, numerous reformist governments challenged the existing distribution of economic power and welfare only to fall victim to economic and political disintegration caused by both their own inadequacies and the retaliatory actions of threatened upper and middle classes. In most countries,[1] these experiences have given way to authoritarian military régimes whose imposition of political controls and conservative development strategies for the most part has been stoically endured by their subject populations. In those escaping military rule,[2] reformist policies and programmes have been abandoned as incompatible with adequate economic growth and stability, again without evoking much resistance or upheaval; while in those recently returning to civilian rule,[3] voters have supported one-time progressives now advocating frankly conservative development strategies (wage restraints, reduced government programmes, and ample incentives for the private sector). Only Nicaragua

56

and Jamaica appear, at the moment, to be moving in progressive directions, and they may simply be at earlier stages of evolution but headed for the same fate.

While one should not ignore the inhibiting impact of restrictive political controls and often brutal repression, the fact that opposition and resistance to such régimes and policies have not been more intense or widespread reflects emerging neo-conservative sentiment among élites and citizens. A substantial number of Latin Americans, including some workers and peasants, appear willing to blame current conditions and difficulties on the Utopianism, sectarianism, and organisational inadequacies of earlier popular movements. Most have lowered their expectations regarding equality and participation, and some are rethinking their political convictions and loyalties. They are more respectful of the strength of 'the system', and are hoping to share, albeit marginally, in the growth and stability being sought by the régimes currently in power. For their part, erstwhile progressive parties and movements are also moving rightwards, hoping to distance themselves from 'the left' and to become more respectable and acceptable in military and financial circles.

2. NEO-CONSERVATISM WITHIN THE CHURCH

These developments have greatly affected the Latin American Church, where sentiments of scepticism, resignation, and aversion to politics can also be detected. This was most recently apparent during the February 1979 Latin American Bishops' Conference (CELAM) at Puebla, where forces opposed to the Church's radicalisation and increased political involvement of recent years sought to redirect its energies into less controversial, more internally oriented areas of pastoral ministry.

The materials prepared for the Conference by CELAM's conservative Secretariat[4] pressed a notion of evangelisation conceived in terms of revelation and religious culture. In an attempt to dilute the critical concern for social structures and relationships fostered at CELAM's Medellín Conference in 1968, they focused on the growing 'secularisation' of Latin American life, to which Catholic values and traditions should be an antidote and alternative (but which Church involvement in secular matters had actually reinforced). 'Reculturation' was to be achieved by a strengthening of Church structures and hierarchy, by the encouragement of popular religiosity, and by renewed emphasis on religious education, preaching, personal prayer, and liturgical devotion. The Church's social mission, though by no means abandoned, would consist in outlining the general values in line with which lay men and women would make particular determination in accord with their own ideological and policy preferences.

These notions were widely debated prior to and at Puebla. The final Conference document retained much of the preparatory versions, but placed greater emphasis on the oppressive socio-economic and political structures in relation to which evangelisation needed to take place. Additionally, it softened criticisms of liberation theology and general social activism, and reaffirmed the popular base communities of which earlier materials had been openly sceptical. It was a compromise document in which the fears, concerns, and priorities of both progressives and conservatives found expression. Its immediate impact has been to confirm people in the pastoral strategies and activities they had previously chosen, although its broader significance is considerably less clear.

The question of how thorough-going this neo-conservative sentiment within the Church is can be partially clarified by looking at the writings of two leading figures of the anti-radical movement: Belgian Jesuit Roger Vekemans, a sociologist and theologian who directs the Centre of Latin American Development and Integration (CEDIAL) in Bogota, Colombia; and Colombian Archbishop Alfonso Lopez Trujillo, formerly (1972-79) CELAM's influential Secretary-General, and now its President. Each played

E

a major role in shaping the preparatory documents, and while neither is a full-fledged neo-conservative in the North American sense of the term, both espouse views and sentiments of an eminently neo-conservative character.

Vekemans has been an influential force within the Latin American Church for over twenty years. In the 1960s, in Chile, he helped develop European-style Catholic social organisations to counter the growing appeal of Marxist groups, later helped design the Frei government's *Promocion Popular* (a programme aimed at integrating 'marginal' sectors of the population into national life), and was an early critic of left-wing Christian Democrats whose impatience with 'bland' Catholic social teaching led them to embrace Marxism and abandon party ranks in 1969. Moving to Bogota in 1970, he has continued to write and speak extensively on the Church, society and politics, and publishes a journal, *Tierra Nueva*, in which extensive critiques of dependence theory, liberation and political theology, and Christianity and Marxism are regularly featured.

Fr Vekemans sees efforts to radicalise the Church as theologically and politically unsound. In his view, neither liberation nor political theology keeps the transcendental dimension of Christian faith in proper perspective; they permit the enterprises of civilisation and social liberation to become preconditions or surrogates (rather than prefigurations) of evangelisation and salvation (*Iglesia y Mundo Politico*, pp. 12-29; and *Tierra Nueva*, #17, p. 18); and in reducing the faith to political praxis, they allow theology to be displaced by social analysis (*op. cit.*, pp. 17 and 31).

Politically, Vekemans sees each deriving its praxiological understanding from a 'Utopianism' which is analytically unsound and replete with potentially dangerous implications. He charges liberation theologians with adopting an analytical framework (Marxism) at odds with Christian principles, and with having done so uncritically, mistaking assertions and interpretation for sociological fact (*Tierra Nueva*, #17, p. 23). And he further argues that the Utopianism of liberation and political theologians is susceptible to totalitarian impulses, overly negative in tone and content, inclined to view as feasible what is humanly impossible, and offering solutions disproportionately vague for so radical a critique (*Iglesia y Mundo Politico*, p. 74).

Vekemans contends that Christian radicals fail to differentiate between the doctrinal, ideological, and policy stages of political reflection. In his view, gospel values should inform doctrinal statements about the nature and moral purposes of social phenomena, but should be applied to concrete situations indirectly, through the mediation of ideological and political criteria, and then not by the Church or its priests, whose mission is to forge unity among its members at a level beyond the divisions inevitably attending such matters (*Iglesia y Mundo Politico*, p. 93).

In contrast, he argues, radicals first distort Catholic social ideals (reformulating them in the light of praxis), and then fail to confine them to the proper level of generality, i.e., they impose them directly on social phenomena, oblivious to the complexity and contingencies of political life, and to the need to adjust standards to the limiting considerations of feasibility, probability, and practical consequences. As a result, they relativise and misappropriate Christian values, and yet fail to treat social reality with the critical attention it deserves.

This is an interesting critique, and possibly appropriate in the case of some liberation theologies. In as much as it is directed at all liberation and political theologians, however, one wonders how anyone with whom Vekemans disagrees ideologically or politically could escape disqualification under its terms. Moreover, Vekemans, is caught in a dilemma. On the one hand, he insists that Catholic social doctrine constitutes a solid and unequivocal body of principles (freedom, justice, equality, participation, etc.) binding on social reality, and not to be twisted or neutralised by ideological sleight of hand. As we shall see, he asserts and defends these in ways and contexts that contravene important neo-conservative positions. But in attacking 'Utopianism' he releases concrete political judgments from the direct hold of moral principles, making them depend on intervening ideological and political understandings, a practice for which he chides radicals, but in which he himself engages in challenging them.

The neo-conservatism emerging somewhat subtley in Fr Vekemans is more fully manifest in Monsignor Lopez Trujillo. Lopez is the young (44), intellectually able, seemingly tireless[5] former auxiliary Bishop of Bogota whom most observers credit with (or condemn for) managing the Puebla process and conference, influencing the composition of various national delegations, and lobbying widely in an effort to arrest the radicalisation of the post-Medellín period. Like Vekemans, his objections are theological and political. He shares Vekemans' view that the proper concern of the Church and its priests is the evangelisation, not the social liberation of the Latin American people. And he further concurs that faith and revelation are principally concerned with *metanoia* (in terms of which Christians are united regardless of their political divisions and differences) and are prior to praxis, i.e., can be understood and communicated without the mediation of ideological or political commitment.

More interesting, however, are Lopez' political judgments. As does Vekemans, he finds the radicalism of progressives 'unrealistic', judgmental rather than analytical, and often merely a badge of courage for those wishing to 'prove' their sophistication, their social sensibility, and their love for the poor (*Criterio*, pp. 701-702). Further, he finds the socialism invoked by most radicals to involve all sorts of problems (e.g., coerciveness and inefficiencies in both the planning and operations phases of the national economy), and urges that in proposing 'bold reforms' one should only go as far as is 'possible, sensible, and useful'. '. . . One cannot simply proceed to show the Christian kindness of (certain) reforms or stages, without substantial dialogue with the experts, and the warnings outlined here oblige us to reflect on the complexity of the phenomena involved and the secondary and political consequences of the radical changes, adjustments, and reforms required . . .' (*Tierra Nueva*, #22, p. 95).

Monsignor Lopez seems as much concerned, moreover, with existing political conditions and relations, and urges a more conciliatory attitude towards Latin American governments. He views the emergence and intensification of authoritarian régimes as having been facilitated by the chaos and social tensions encouraged by radical movements, and in some instances by units of the Church itself (*Criterio*, p. 702). In his view, continued radical activism would perpetuate tensions between Church and State, preventing either from carrying out its mission. Such tensions, he writes, '. . . represent an obstacle to both evangelisation and the task of social cohesion which governments should be furthering. . . . The prophetic presence of the Church will be more substantial and attractive when it avoids having its positions appear politically oppositional'. And therefore, '. . . If it is true . . . that one of the contributions of the Church is the Christian formation of conscience in terms of social commitment, one should not aggravate (*extremar*) tensions. One should (rather) hold out bridges and channels of dialogue' (*Criterio*, p. 702).

3. SOCIO-ECONOMIC AND CULTURAL OBSTACLES

Their theological and political Augustinianism notwithstanding, however, Vekemans and Lopez Trujillo fail to qualify as full-fledged neo-conservatives in the North American sense of the term. Neither finds hidden or ultimately vindicating virtue in existing social conditions, nor is either willing for the Church to turn entirely inward, abandoning society or the political order to their appointed fates.

Conspicuously absent from the thinking of both, for example, is any enthusiasm for the virtues of capitalism or the free market. While North American neo-conservatives regard these as the indispensable bases for freedom and prosperity, Vekemans and Lopez, influenced by Catholic social teaching, are instead highly critical of capitalism's underlying values and motivation, the pattern and level of development to which it leads, and the adverse impact it often has on individual and social freedom.

Vekemans denies that capitalist growth feeds off the exploitation of Latin America's 'marginal' population, but insists that it is incapable of bringing that sector effectively into the national economy or society (*Tierra Nueva*, #2, pp. 58-59). For his part, Lopez Trujillo holds capitalism responsible for 'having produced an offensive concentration of wealth and opportunities against, and at the expense of others, on whom it imposes its laws and conditions' (*Tierra Nueva*, #22, p. 86).

This hostility to capitalism is not just a reflection of loyalty to Catholic social teaching. It is also a conclusion to which Vekemans and Lopez Trujillo are drawn by capitalism's historical performance in Latin America, where it has neither freedom nor prosperity to show for its years of profitable operation.

A central claim of North American neo-conservatism is that the growth and profitability of an unrestricted private sector contributes more to the material well-being of the poor and working class than to high taxes, restrictive controls and wars on poverty and unemployment. Unfortunately, the 'trickle down' logic on which the claim rests has never been an easy one to sell in Latin America. There, under even the best of circumstances, i.e., when high rates of growth in GNP have been sustained over long periods of time (e.g., Mexico and Brazil), income differentials have increased, and in some cases poverty and unemployment have actually grown more widespread, prompting one Head of State to concede that the economy had done well but the people poorly.

Capitalism's record has been so poor in Latin America, in fact, that its advocacy may not be a politically viable option for anyone, neo-conservative or otherwise, interested in developing or retaining a broad popular following. The economic and social conditions which it has produced are simply not 'well enough' to be left alone. Too many people are without food, jobs, and shelter, for Latin Americans to take consolation or refuge in an untrammelled private sector and free market.

The other side of the neo-conservative argument, that private ownership of the means of production provides an essential foundation for the exercise of personal and social freedom, is similarly implausible in the Latin American context. Whatever its record elsewhere, Latin American capitalism has made no such contribution. It has pursued and sought to preserve its interests not by opposing the State and its power, but by purchasing its complicity and repressive services, thus further restricting the enjoyment of freedom.

Given the Latin American experience under capitalism, one would also not expect governments and government programmes to be as readily or blithely maligned as elsewhere. But, in addition, there are deeply-rooted cultural attitudes and values that prevent Latin American neo-conservatives from summoning up the same anti-State sentiment as their North American counterparts. Neither the private entrepreneur nor the rugged individual enjoys the reverence or symbolic stature in Latin America that they do in Anglo-Saxon culture, whereas the State and government have long been central and respected features of social life, on which people are encouraged to rely for assistance and protection, not fly from out of fear or self-respect.[6]

A final factor inhibiting neo-conservative sentiment within the Church in particular is the harrassment and persecution to which it has been subjected by hostile governments and political forces. The connection between political adversity and religious fervour is a powerful one, and religious institutions will probably always serve as sources of refuge and consolation to the weary and oppressed. But repression and persecution can also reach a point at which the Church can no longer remain passive and detached, and must become an agency of active defence and resistance. In effect, when the Church's own institutions and personnel, or the people entrusted to its ministry, are attacked or pursued, there is no longer a private realm to which to retreat.

The radicalising potential of such circumstances is dramatically illustrated in the case of the late Archbishop Oscar Romero of El Salvador. At the time of his appointment (1977), he was widely regarded as a conservative, but in the three years before his death he became the Church's leading advocate of active involvement in defence of the poor and oppressed, whatever the consequences. Indeed, Fr Vekemans himself acknowledges that the Church's concern for its own (higher) unity in no way permits it to remain 'apolitical'. Pointing to the historically disastrous consequences of such an attitude (the case of Nazi Germany), he writes: '. . . Unity achieved by means of abandoning commitments is a fictitious, empty unity. . . . Men are its (the Church's) human commitments. To bring them together by leaving commitments outside is to bring them together in terms of something other than what they are, it is to bring together phantasms' (*Tierra Nueva*, #5, p. 48).

4. NEO-CONSERVATISM AND CHRISTIAN DEMOCRACY

Socio-economic, cultural, and political factors of Latin American life thus militate against either Vekemans or Lopez Trujillo adopting a more thorough-going neo-conservatism. Put somewhat differently, they make it difficult for Latin American neo-conservatives, whether within or beyond the Church, to embrace attitudes towards capitalism and social responsibility typical of other neo-conservative movements. These factors were no doubt at work at Puebla, and played a role in the passage of amendments reaffirming the essential insights of Medellín. They will probably also exert a restraining influence on neo-conservative sentiment within the Church in the months and years to come.

It is likely, for example, that neo-conservatives within the Church will continue to oppose both liberal capitalism and State socialism, and to call for a 'Third Way' alternative in the manner of European and Latin American Christian Democracy. What this will mean concretely will depend on socio-economic trends, changing political contexts, and whether this anti-capitalism becomes (or remains) genuine or rhetorical. Many would argue that it has remained rhetorical in the vast majority of Christian Democratic experiences, that 'Third Way' approaches have been noteworthy for their resistance to, not support of structural changes, and that their concern for reconciling or harmonising divergent class interests effectively assures continued capitalist hegemony. Vekemans and Lopez might argue that they neither intend nor would sanction such things. But as they would hold radicals accountable for the practical costs and consequences of their Utopian schemes, so must they answer for those of their own.

An interesting question in this connection concerns how such progressive, 'Christian Democratic' neo-conservatives would respond if economic growth under free enterprise capitalism, even though the fruit of unrestrained material self interest, were to begin 'trickling down' after all. Strictly speaking, the coincidence between narrow self-interest and broader social benefits should be of little consolation to either Christian Democrats or adherents of Catholic social teaching. And yet the matter may be ideologically negotiable. One's ability to detect the presence of narrowly self-interested motives may prove to vary inversely with the extent of generalised prosperity, and where this were significant (the case of most developed countries), it might suddenly be easier to see (and applaud) the social consciousness of the entrepreneurial class.

This susceptibility to opportunistic interpretation and application has long been a major liability of 'Third Way' postures. In effect, they offer a theoretical reconciliation of individual and collective values that can both accommodate and legitimise systematic subordination of the latter. The potential for this seems substantial with Vekemans and Lopez, and could underwrite an extension of neo-conservatism beyond that expressed or intended in their theoretical positions.

In the meantime, under Lopez' leadership, CELAM continues its push against radical forces and influence. Recent reflections of this include reported efforts to dilute the progressive character of the Brazilian Bishops' Conference by recommending conservatives to fill episcopal vacancies, and to have CELAM itself, not the Nicaraguan bishops, co-ordinate all external economic assistance to Church projects in that country. The anti-radical offensive seems to have considerable Vatican support. It is rooted in an ecclesiology conditioned by the same neo-conservatism as is apparent in Vekemans and Lopez Trujillo, and will no doubt have a conservative impact on the role of the Church within society, and perhaps on the thinking of individual Catholics as well.

Notes

1. Chile, Brazil, Argentina, Uruguay, Ecuador, Bolivia and Peru (post 1975).
2. Mexico, Costa Rica, Colombia and Venezuela.
3. Ecuador, Bolivia, the Dominican Republic and Peru.
4. There were two documents, the initial Document of Consultation, widely referred to as the 'preparatory document', and a subsequently revised 'working document', which attempted to accommodate some of the criticism directed at the first.
5. Lopez is said to have made an average of two trips per month to Rome during the year preceding the Puebla Conferences.
6. See Glen C. Dealy *The Public Man* (Amherst, Mass. 1977).

References

Vekemans, Roger *Iglesia y Mundo Politico* (Barcelona 1971). 'Unidad y pluralismo en la Iglesia' *Tierra Nueva* 5 (1973) 45-50. 'Panoramica actual de la teologia de la liberacion en America Latina *Tierra Nueva* 17 (1976) 5-33.

Vekemans, Roger and Duran, Fernando, G.y. 'Marginalidad y desarrollo' *Tierra Nueva* 2 (1972) 50-62.

Trujillo, Alfonso Lopez 'Diez Anos Despues de Populoroum Progressio' *Tierra Nueva* 22 (1977). 'La Iglesia en America Latina' *Criterio* (1977) 699-704.

André Rousseau

On the 'Crisis' of Progressivism among French Catholics— Clarifications and Hypotheses

IN 1970 a mass circulation weekly widely read by the managerial class ran as its cover title 'The Church Swings Left'. Ten years later the same magazine was less categorical and, in an issue entitled 'Catholics and Politics', showed that this 'swing' had, in the end, affected only a minority.[1] Indeed, one of the two main features highlighted by all the professional observations is that while, from the beginning of the 1960s to the middle of the 1970s, the proportion of Catholics—practising Catholics alone—voting for the parties of the left markedly increased, this development took place in the context of an increase of support for these parties among the electorate as a whole. The other feature is that it is not possible to make a simple equation between a 'swing to the left' on the part of Catholics and a vote for the Socialist Party—the only one to increase its support markedly among the Catholic electorate. The reason for this is that this party which, since 1971, has been uniting various tendencies to which Catholic activists had made contributions, no longer represents, as it once did, the anti-clerical version of secular humanism. To talk of the 'progressivism of Catholics' in France may therefore give rise to a false view of the situation, both quantitatively and qualitatively.

1. PROGRESSIVE CATHOLICS

Certainly for non-French readers, the term 'progressivism' applied to French Catholics very probably implies an openness on their part which distinguishes them to some extent from other Roman Catholics. It is therefore necessary to make clear that the phenomenon denoted by the term 'progressivism', while diverse and complex, also has a much more definite shape than what is usually described by the word because it is connected historically with the political situation of the years 1930-50. In this period the discussions about 'Christian progressivism' centred on three interdependent questions. One was the place of the working class, its organisations and goals in the movement (or, in the language of the time, the 'direction') of history. The second was the problem of collaboration with the Communist Party and/or its mass organisations such as the Peace Movement. The third was the question of the use of Marxism in the interpretation of society and in the expression of Christian identity.

These three issues, while in themselves closely connected, were not all equally important for all the elements of this activist movement. The third, in particular, was far from arousing wide interest. It seems to have been discussed, or at least raised, mainly by priests in the groups and periodicals labelled 'progressive'.[2] The local hierarchy, however, like the Holy See and the Holy Office, together with a number of theologians, assessed all these movements solely in terms of 'doctrinal deviations'.[3] 'Progressivism' in the strict sense was thus, in Catholic circles, a label covering numerically insignificant groups in which workers were no more than a sizeable minority alongside intellectuals and clergy.[4] Without being over-schematic, we can say that these movements were responsible for the movement from a 'social Catholicism' to a socialist politics inspired by the working-class movement and pursued by Catholics who belonged neither to the traditional élites nor to the 'de-Christianised' proletariat. Through the period from the 'Popular Front' (1936) to the Resistance (1940-44) they had experienced the ties between the working-class movement and the 'people' with which, for religious reasons, they were anxious to 'make contact'. But in taking this path these movements were destined almost inevitably to come into contact with the ecclesiastical authorities in so far as, in the eyes of the latter, they were diverting the Catholic movement from its goals. Thirty years ago Père Montuclard wrote, 'The JOC was told in the past and Mission Ouvrière is being told again today: You are letting yourselves be contaminated. Instead of proclaiming the gospel you are encouraging class struggle. . . . And today's apostles, like the *Jocistes* of the past, answer, "What gospel do you want us to proclaim? The one which in practice covers up the compromises of Christians and the clergy with a régime against which we are fighting? For us there is only one attitude which is authentic and possible: to keep quiet . . . and take part in the life, in all the struggles, in all the latent culture of that working population. . . ! We have even abandoned the aim of converting . . .".'[5] Inevitably, such language drew both verbal and practical sanctions. In the Fifties, faced with the doctrinal declarations of the progressive movement, the bishops revived Action Catholique Ouvrière (Catholic Action among the Working Class) to 'summon the Christians of the working-class world to a positive task of evangelisation among the popular masses and to an educative mission among them in the light of the Church's social teaching'.[6]

2. HISTORICAL EVOLUTION

The development of the discussion about 'progressive Catholicism'—and of all the various issues—since the period of 1930-50 can in my view be best judged under four complementary heads: the transformation of the political arena, the debates on the role (and the functions) of the working class, increasing cultural differences among Catholics and the 'rise' of the new middle classes and lastly the distribution of power within Catholicism. In one sense each of the elements to some extent implies the others and I distinguish them for convenience of exposition.

Various developments in the transformation of the political arena need to be considered. First, to take only the most visible features, while the working-class organisations and the left-wing parties have absorbed an increasing number of Catholics, the main beneficiaries of this influx into the political arena have been the trade unions, above all the former 'Christian trade union', the CFTC, which became a secular organisation in 1964 with the new name 'Confédération Française Démocratique du Travail' (CFDT). For many Catholic activists the CFTC/CFDT has provided an indirect way into political activity, especially through its role in formulating the ideas which were to contribute in the Sixties to the formation of a non-communist left. Many observers note that Catholics have formed a distinct element in the recent ideological development of the working-class movement,[7] where their idealist and 'moral' concerns—an obvious example is the movement for workers' control—have begun to become practicable demands among the fragments of new classes or groups with what might be called confused class positions, such as office workers, minor officials, technical and highly skilled workers. As a result Catholics have become quite closely involved in two not entirely complementary developments. On the one hand there is the appearance of political issues outside the 'parties'. An exception which confirms the rule here is the *Parti Socialiste Unifié* (PSU), formed in 1960 by Catholic activists,[8] and former activists of the Communist Party and the SFIO,[9] the first suspicious of Stalinism and the second of the reformism and the colonial policies of the parties of the non-communist left.[10] On the other hand, these groups eventually helped to establish the new *Parti Socialiste* in 1971, when a sizable minority of PSU activists (including the Catholics who had been brought up on the progressive Christianity of the Forties and Fifties) combined with former activists of the MRP[11] During the same period the Communist Party was fundamentally revising its analyses of religious phenomena and, between the end of the 1960s to 1978, made frequent gestures in the direction of the 'mass of Christians' as part of its policy, promoted most vigorously from 1972 onwards, of a 'union of the French people' against monopoly capitalism.

This strategy of the Communist Party was in direct line of succession to the policy of 'an open hand to the Catholics' (in Maurice Thorez' phrase of 1936), but broadened it in various ways. First it was based on a sort of fundamental principle of support for the positions of the Catholic hierarchy and, more generally, of the clergy and the Catholic Action movements. More important for the subject of this article, however, is the fact that the Communist Party's view was no longer that it was principally 'working-class and white-collar Catholics, artisans and shopkeepers' who were regarded as potential allies of working-class movement, but 'Christians in general'. In contrast, however, the Christians who would have been called 'progressive' in the Fifties in the historical sense of the term were now regarded by the French CP with a mixture of puzzlement and suspicion. The reasons for this seem to me to fall into two groups.

First, these heirs of the 'Progressive Christians' were very close to, or even themselves were, the originators of theories of society which appeared in the Sixties and more or less fundamentally revised the Marxist schema of the opposition between bourgeoisie and proletariat.[12] The issue at the centre of this theoretical and ideological battle over the frontiers of social classes was largely, or even exclusively, the competition of the political and union organisations in the area of the 'middle classes'. By introducing novelties such as ideas of a 'new working class' into the Marxist theory of classes, intellectuals forced the Communist Party to revise a view which had regarded managers as almost parasitical groups. In addition its vision of the 'middle-range wage-earning groups' was matched on its left by the theory of the 'new petty bourgeoisie', accompanied by an elaborate theory of classes linked to the political theme of the union of the French people. . . . Now, as it happens, the Catholics who were more or less the direct heirs of the progressives belonged in their overwhelming majority to those social strata which fell between the historical classifications and the historical parties. The intellectuals of these movements, in particular, through the PSU and through the various 'leftist' groups produced by May 1968, offered political alternatives to the so-called 'Union of the Left' and the Common Programme produced by the Communist Party and the *Parti Socialiste* in 1972. The entry of large numbers of Catholic activists into the *Parti Socialiste* in 1971 made no difference in this respect to the relations of progressive Catholics with the French Communist Party. The effect was much more the reverse, since with them certain forms of 'political idealism' became established in the Union of the Left, bringing into it the competition which had previously existed between the CFDT and the CGT.[13]

At the same time it was not pure coincidence that these Catholics were also those who in the Sixties and Seventies went a very long way in exploring the place of Marxist philosophy in their interpretation of society and the Church and in the expression of their Christian identity. They had had to produce their own political ideas, all the more because the Church's official line had been opposition no less to liberalism than to socialism, though it may also be permissible to see this discovery of Marxism as a sort of breach created in the monopoly of a party not one's own and even possible to see it as a sort of transfer of habits, Marxist coherence giving a political tint to Catholic theology's fondness for systems. . . . There seem to me to be two points which deserve consideration here. First of all the Marxism of the progressive Catholics of the Seventies was a university Marxism which would not have had the success it had if it had not found a hyper-educated constituency ready to accept its apparatus of scientificity and so confirmed in its sense of being Marxist in the 'right way', not disciples of 'vulgar Marxism', 'mechanistic Marxism' and so on. But what made it even more difficult for these Catholics to be accepted as comrades by the French communists was the fact that by blurring the frontiers between Marxism and Christianity they were likely to introduce 'noise' into the 'dialogue' between comparable institutions with clear boundaries. Now these Catholics were no longer content to 'put a red bonnet on the dictionary' (in this case of Catholic Theology); they also introduced novelties of vocabulary and even syntax. And there was also the problem that between the Christians who were members of the Communist Party and those who called themselves Marxists without being Party members there existed a sort of rivalry to define the right way of being both a Marxist and a Christian.

3. A MINORITY

There is yet another element of confusion.[14] Activists belonging to the working class, or claiming to belong to it, and grouped together in Action Catholique Ouvrière, display firm resistance both to the hyper-coherence which leads the progressive intellectuals to make everything, including religious language, into a political problem and to the temptation to set up a movement of 'Christians for Socialism'. This gulf can be understood if one makes an effort to define and compare the aims of the two groups. The 'intellectuals', the successors of the progressive Catholics of the past, start from the beginning by taking up a position in the area of religious legitimacy: they present themselves as an alternative authority and tend to define themselves as the guardians of the true Christian tradition. In contrast, the working-class movements within Catholic Action demonstrate a division of power: the priests appointed to these movements have gradually been given an area of their own by the hierarchy. Within that area semantic changes have taken place in such ideas as evangelisation, witness, liberation and so on which as far as possible reconcile Christian interpretations and those which derive from the ideologies of the working-class movement. In this transaction lay activists are regarded by their organisations as really Catholic and at the same time fully involved in the working-class movement.

Nevertheless, all that has just been described represents no more than an active and influential minority within French Catholicism, and one whose weight in the Church system could well decrease in the near future. It cannot be denied that this historical grouping of priests and laity linked to the left-wing parties and the trade-union movement raised the issue of political pluralism in French Catholicism in terms which forced the bishops to address Catholics as a whole on the problems defined by this active minority. This was in 1972, during a period when the Union of the Left was particularly strong. Nevertheless, in 1975 the question of the right of Catholic Action to take political positions was treated in the context of an insistence by the bishops that Catholic movements are an extension of their own action on society and, as such, make 'political options' only at their discretion. The extreme fragmentation of the movements and the ideological and cultural divisions between them weaken their position in such a situation. Nor do the declining hopes of political change since 1978 make things any better.

Translated by Francis McDonagh

Notes

1. *L'Express* 5 December 1970 and 5 April 1980.
2. I give a list of the various elements of a whole without specifying sometimes important nuances: The journal *Esprit*, founded by Mounier in 1932; the weekly *Sept*, founded by Dominicans and lay people in 1934 closed in 1937 and 'succeeded' by *Temps Présent* (which disappeared with the war); *Terre Nouvelle* ('the organ of revolutionary Christians'), written by both Catholics and Protestants, condemned in 1936; Mouvement de Libération du Peuple (1950), a product of a split in one of the Catholic Action movements (the Mouvement Populaire des Familles) consisting of former members of JOC; *Jeunesse de l'Eglise*, a series started by a team of lay people and Dominicans in 1941; *Témoignage Chrétien*, a periodical founded during the Resistance (1940) which became a weekly under the same title at the Liberation. In founding *Economie et Humanisme* in the same period, Père Lebret envisaged a centre for studies of Marxism. 1947 saw the setting up of the Union des Chrétiens Progressistes, 1950 the appearance of *La Quinzaine*, a journal condemned in 1954 by the French bishops and in 1955 by Rome, which became *La Lettre* in 1957.
3. See P. Bigo 'Le progressisme, aspects doctrinaux' *Revue de l'Action Populaire* (May 1955); esp. G. Fessard *De l'actualité historique, II. Progressisme chrétien et apostolat ouvrier* (Paris 1960), with Mgr Guerry's reply to the author's criticisms of the bishops' lack of firmness towards Marxist influence of the Catholic workers' movements, 'Progressisme chrétien et apostolat dans le monde ouvrier' *La Documentation Catholique* (1960), LVIII, No. 1337, cols. 1217-1231. The same scene was replayed in 1979 after the publication of a posthumous work by the same Père Fessard (a founder of *Témoignage Chrétien*!): *Eglise de France, prends garde de perdre la foi*. See the reply by Mgr Maziers 'Exigences du service de l'Evangile en monde ouvrier' *L'Aquitaine. Semaine religieuse de l'Archidiocèse de Bordeaux* 37, 19 October 1979, 439-496.
4. Including many 'worker priests' and members of the Mission de France.
5. M. Montuclard *Les Evénements et la Foi. Jeunesse de l'Eglise* (Paris 1951) p. 60.
6. Mgr Guerry in the article cited in note 3, col. 1224.
7. See esp. F. Bédarida and J. Matron *Christianisme et monde ouvrier* (Paris 1975) pp. 11-34.
8. Largely from the Union des Chrétiens Progressistes and the MRP (see above, note 2).
9. The old-style Socialist Party which resulted from an internal split in the Communist Party in 1920.
10. The Indo-China war was not far off and the Algerian Revolution was at its height.
11. The Mouvement Républicain Populaire, with a Christian Democrat leadership, markedly more left-wing activists and a majority of right-wing voters—all or nearly all Catholics!
12. See their journals *Cité Nouvelle* and *La Lettre*. They are also to be found in a less radical form (verbally at least) among the readers of *Témoignage Chrétien*, the members of Vie Nouvelle,

of the Equipes Enseignantes, the Mouvement Rural de la Jeunesse Chrétienne (the former JAC), the readers of *Notre Combat*, the members of the Cercle Jean XXIII, the readers of *Cultures et Foi*, the members of the Jeunesse Etudiante Chrétienne. This list is not meant to imply that all the members of the organisations mentioned can be placed in the same ideological category. To the list may be added a group such as the Catholic Committee Against Hunger and For Development, many of whose organisers and activists adopted a more radical political position as a result of study of the international relationships of domination.

13. The CGT is by far the largest manual workers' union and the most deeply rooted in the oldest sectors of the working class. The CFDT has more success among workers who are 'new' in the sense that they have just left agriculture or craft occupations or in the sense that they have positions and qualifications of recent appearance in the productive system (e.g., office workers, postal and telecommunications workers, etc.). It has also been adapted better to the problems of immigrant workers.

14. I have developed the following point in 'Chrétiens pour le Socialisme et Action Catholique Ouvrière en France: deux stratégies socio-religieuses' *Social Compass* 25 (1972) No. 1 101-113.

Dorothee Sölle

The Repression of the Existential Element, or Why So Many People become Conservative

'PHONE US—ANY TIME.' We found this message beside the telephone one night and the number given was that of a students' residence. If we had found it at the end of the 1960s, the context would certainly have been political—a demonstration, leaflets or steps to be taken to help those who were being persecuted. At the end of the 1970s, we would have thought at once of a psychological problem—a student was suffering from depression or contemplating an abortion or suicide. In the summer of 1980, the reason for this phone message was quite different—a passionate discussion about the meaning of life between one and four o'clock in the morning, to which a group of a dozen students wanted to invite their teacher.

What was this really about? These young men and women are not neo-conservatives. They take part in demonstrations against nuclear energy, the reactionary candidates for the chancellorship and the right wing. What is new in this case is that they are concerned with philosophy and that they express needs that have to do with metaphysics, absolute claims and the meaning of life. They feel that they have been left alone with these needs in our technocratic consumer society—abandoned and misunderstood by both the old and the new left-wing.

One of the last great attempts made in Europe to deal with the questions that present themselves only very vaguely and timidly today was the movement known as existentialism and there are good reasons for believing that it may be revived quite soon. In 1978, Jürgen Habermas called on some fifty or so criticis, authors and scientists, including three theologians, to define their position with regard to the 'spiritual situation of the present time', in memory of the book of that title written by Karl Jaspers almost fifty years ago.[1]

Rereading Jaspers' book, I wondered what was really meant by the category 'unconditional existential aspect' and what Jaspers in particular meant by it. I also wondered whether there was also a need for such an unconditional aspect today and whether we had the linguistic apparatus with which to express it. I also asked myself whether the theological background to this question could be in any way illuminated. Finally, I wondered whether traditional religious language could help at all in our understanding of the spiritual and political situation of the 1980s.

Jaspers criticised the 'universal existential apparatus' that oppresses us in the interest of a 'concrete human world'. He claimed that 'if man no longer produces, fashions and hands down anything in the concrete world that surrounds him, but simply accepts, uses and exchanges everything as satisfying his immediate needs and if he makes his habitation entirely by machine, banishes the spirit from his environment, regards work simply as achievement from day to day and constructs nothing at all for the purpose of a life—he would, so to speak, be without a world'.[2]

These words were written long before the second industrial revolution took place and they have therefore lost their critical character. There has, for instance, been a further decrease in the number of people who produce, fashion or hand anything down. The 'spirit of man's own environment' can only be seen now as a caricature, because it has become completely privatised in the form of a second home on the Mediterranean coast. The 'continuity' of man's personality was ridiculed by Gottfried Benn and is 'guaranteed by the suits that last for ten years if the material is good'.

In answer to the question as to what might save man from the apparatus or what might keep his world human or make it human again, Jaspers provides a number of formal phrases, such as 'coming to being' (p. 39), the 'movement up to real humanity' (p. 68) and above all the 'unconditional existential aspect' which keeps man's 'claim to existence' alive (p. 40).

All these formulae strike one now as remarkably empty and, even if they have some content, they have become debased to the level of a criticism of society, directed mainly against Marxism and psychoanalysis and combined together with an attack against racism and given the generic name of the criticism of ideology. Quite apart from this unfounded and élitist criticism of mass existence, however, one important question still remains unanswered. It is this: Do the formulae which Jaspers used and his perhaps too grandiose statements about man's 'fate' and his 'real humanity' perhaps not hide more than the fears felt among the middle classes in Germany during the 1930s of a loss of prestige with which the mass culture threatened them? Jaspers was perhaps looking for something, in his analysis of the 'unconditional existential aspect', that was viewed at that time with suspicion as 'irrationalism' and was at the same time apparently more than a mere negation of critical reason.

What is this 'unconditioned' element? It is at least an interest in an existence that is not absorbed into the functions for others that it fulfils and is not merely a means for other ends determined by others. Existence is the title below which this element that cannot be reduced, inferred or made into a function appears. Existence is therefore the fundamental term in a philosophy of liberation that is opposed to the functionalisation of man's life in the great apparatuses of society. 'I exist' means: 'I am no longer simply the object of others. I am more than they know about me. I am more than they can use. Even if I know myself to be conditioned in every way, the meaning of my life is to be an end and not simply a means, to exist and not simply to function.'

However value-conservative or even partly reactionary Jaspers' conclusions may strike us when seen in this light, there is still a need to make a distinction, within existential philosophy, between emancipative and humanistic elements and repressive and élitist elements. The claim to exist, to be an end and not simply a means and to fulfil an 'existence' and not merely a function is one of man's deepest human needs, which cannot be satisfied by being denied as 'irrational'. To call it unconditional and absolute may perhaps be misleading, because this unconditional aspect can only take place under certain conditions that can be investigated and inferred and the absolute aspect can only be understood if its relativity is ascertained. This does not in any way determine the question of the unconditional nature and the irreducible meaning of human life.

In history, this question has been expressed in the language of religion. The whole of Jaspers' analysis bears the imprint of a deep sorrow for lost religions. It is, in a sense, a philosophy of the death of God, but it replaces the element for which the word 'God' once stood by 'existential'. Religion was a historical form in which this need for absolute value was expressed in the past and our task is to find another language to express this unconditional element, in which men will be assured of the meaning of their lives, in our post-religious age.

Jaspers attempted to do precisely this. His experience of the 'unconditional existential element' and his clinging to this conviction led him to his 'philosophical faith'. We are, however, bound to ask whether, even within this independent faith that has been detached from the tradition and the institution of the churches, he did not remain more firmly in the grip of religion than he himself knew. Is this excessive demand for meaning, truth and absolute value, however philosophically it may be expressed in Jaspers' writing, not, in the last resort, a part of religion? Would it therefore not be in the best interests of the unconditional existential element to express the religious tradition in contemporary language? We cannot, surely, afford to neglect our accumulated experience with meaning, encountered in Scripture and tradition, when it is a question of presenting and handing on unmediated existential experience?

Jaspers lived at the end of the age of bread, at a time when plastic had not yet become the main item of diet. Religion was becoming extinct, but there was certainly no less need for meaning. The new situation in which we find ourselves confronted with Jaspers can be described in this way: there is no longer any language in which meaning, the unconditional existential element and faith can be made credible. The age of bread is at an end and we may say that even the age of the philosophical roll is over. The needs to which we are currently exposed have been greatly manipulated and even our need to be different, to be made new and to be sure of the meaning of life has been converted into a need to possess. Mastery, the manipulation of man's consciousness and education for the destruction of man's self interests are no longer carried out by religion and the churches, but by production and publicity. The new religion is consumerism. The consumer society has succeeded perfectly in repressing the 'unconditional existential aspect'.

The Italian author and film-maker, Pier Paolo Pasolini, wrote: 'There is in fact nothing religious in the ideal image of the young couple projected by the television. They are simply two persons whose lives are made real only by means of consumer goods. . . .'[3]

What is meant by 'nothing religious' here? Does it mean that the ideal image of the young couple was previously surrounded by a different aura? Was it filled with a different content? Did it hold out a firmer promise of happiness than that provided by consuming goods with each other?

Max Horkheimer said: 'It is vain to try to save an unconditioned meaning without God.' The mythical reason for life that cannot be made and is not given in the material sense is found in the word 'God'. 'Without God' was therefore an illusion because, in the Frankfurt school, as in the case of Jaspers, there is a danger that worldly, partial, conditioned and special ends will spread as though they were universal, unconditioned and divine. Living without God seemed meaningful, but it seemed to contradict rational thought, because it was only possible to reject false gods and idols *with* God. It has to be admitted, of course, that there is always the danger in Horkheimer's philosophy that 'God' is reduced to a mere function, that of purifying, destroying images and criticising ideologies. Positive statements about God's intention, about what side he is on and myths that shed light on our situation and give rise to hope were not possible here, because unconditional meaning was in each case only acquired from the springboard of what conditions.

In the philosophical approach, then, the prohibition of images rather than the exodus from Egypt was adopted. This way could not lead Jaspers out of his difficulties in trying to 'save an unconditioned meaning without God'. The 'unconditional aspect' cannot be achieved without a 'leap', in other words, without a decision for life and against death. To give just one example, in which the 'unconditional existential factor' is given a practical and political slant, there is no 'rational reason' for not ending the lives of weak-minded children.

'Seek first the kingdom of God . . . and all these things (food, drink and clothing are meant here) shall be yours as well' (Matt. 6:33)—this expression of the 'unconditional existential factor' presupposes that it is possible for our life to be whole. There are situations in which we are conscious of being undivided and unseparated and in possession of every ability and dimension (including the past and the future). The oil in the lamps of the virgins waiting for the bridegroom is an image for that wholeness. Without oil, they have nothing at all—they are 'foolish', unprepared and absent-minded. When their lamps are full, they have nothing to worry about and they are quite all right.

The unconditional existential aspect is to be found in the indivisible wholeness in favour of which I decide. 'Choosing life' presupposes that there is 'life' in this emphatic and unconditioned sense and that it can be chosen and seized or else rejected and not possessed. 'I call heaven and earth to witness against you this day, that I have set before you life and death, blessing and curse; therefore choose life, that you and your descendants may live' (Deut. 30:19). Within this tradition, a language was developed in which the emphasis on life, its dangers and its salvation were recalled, made present and in that way made possible.

The integrative aspect ('wholeness') and the voluntative element ('decision') together constitute what Jaspers called the 'unconditional existential aspect'. But, even if this language is traced back to its theological origins, there is still a lingering feeling of unease with regard to it.

In comparison with the language of the Bible, there is a clear formalisation and emptying of content in the case of the language of existential philosophy. Terms such as blessing and curse, good and evil, land and banishment as well as such words as 'lamp', 'wedding' and the 'kingdom of God' all contain a great deal more than such concepts as the 'unconditional existential element'. In a sense, this philosophical language is as weak as the language of adolescents, whose most important positive words are 'really' and 'fabulous'. Existential philosophy impresses on us the need for a non-functional basis for life, but it has not succeeded in doing much more than this. The prevailing phenomenon is that we lack a language which is able to inform us about the meaning of life, man's capacity for truth and the unconditional nature and wholeness of his existence in such a way that these can be intelligible. This lack of a suitable language makes people conservative. It would seem as though a reference to early formulae, traditional rules and familiar values is able to help us to recover our existence, which is threatened by our technological society!

In 1968, the students wrote on Paris walls: 'Survivre n'est pas vivre!' But what is 'living' in this sense? Can it be understood only by being contrasted with 'survival'? Can we say only what we do not want and what does not mean life? Pasolini linked his criticism of the prevalent consumerism, among other things, to the destruction of language and more particularly to the increasing destruction of 'expressive' language. There is still mutual comprehension, but nothing more is expressed. Pasolini believed that man's ability to use this 'expressive' language was above all to be found in dialect and that this ability was eradicated with the disappearance of dialects. The prevalent language was that of television and all other languages—regional languages and those used by different classes and groups—were reduced to the same level and even suppressed by the one television language. This reduction to one single level means the loss of all expressiveness in language. Man no longer communicates himself in this single language and therefore is not able to communicate with others. There is mutual comprehension, but only quite directly and without any roundabout ways. Scientific language has erected a taboo against expressive language and this has made it very difficult for most women to make themselves intelligible to each other, because the language of science is in conflict with the part that they have to play as exponents of expressive language. In speaking an ordinary 'man's' sentence, the speaker has the feeling that he is saying nothing. Television advertisements result in a levelling down of everyday language and encourage the spread of scientific language.

When man loses his ability to use expressive language, he is cut off from every form of transcendence. Pasolini's young couple, whose lives are expressed in the consumption of goods, have, in accordance with the prevailing ethos of the television, no longer any need for a language to express their own sorrows and their own desires. It is not that life itself is at stake, but rather that it is only really worth anything as long as man is able to purchase. It is common to hear American tourists visiting the countries of the eastern bloc saying: 'All these empty shop windows! It is all so dull! It's not worth staying alive!'

Pasolini went so far as to call consumerism a new form of fascism because it was very quietly and without physical violence gradually destroying all human values—simply with its means of communication and its power to inform and publicise. If the age of bread is past, is there any meaning at all in continuing to share bread and wine with each other? 'It is clear,' Pasolini wrote, 'that superfluous goods make life itself super-fluous' (p. 46).

Man's awareness of the fact that his life is at stake and that it can become meaningless has been expressed in all the religious traditions. They have given a name to his fears that he can lose himself and that his life can lose its meaning, fears that can also be manipulated. A prayer that was used for centuries was, significantly, 'Protect us from hell'. It expressed something that nowadays would be regarded as qualifying a man for the psychiatric ward—fear of the loss of life and of the destruction of wholeness. In the midst of life we do not live; in the midst of permanently heated rooms the cold increases—'dead!' is a very common answer when a young person is asked what life was like in a certain place.

It is possible to lose possession of the whole of life—to throw it away, treating it like a 'throw-away' article. It can be lost or won, but it can never be really possessed. In any case, we lack a sufficiently expressive and transcendent language to be able to speak about it with each other. Without this existential fear about life, however, there is no more profound love of life, but only a superficial, quickly and permanently frustrated aggressive mood, which can at any time change into a diffused sadness. It is only possible to love what is endangered and what might also be different or might not be at all. In other words, one cannot love what is dead.

The unconditional existential element goes together with existential fear. Our emphatic understanding of life as continuous development, being touched and touching, growing into a new quality and becoming a different experience—this qualitative understanding of life includes an emphatic and traumatic relationship with death. We are capable of being put to death. It is more important to know this than to keep repeating that we are mortal. It is possible that no one knows this better than those who are suffering from psychological disorder. Life can be lost on the way between birth and death. If this were not so, it could also not be won.

If, within the Judaeo-Christian tradition, life has always been at stake and has always had the emphatic significance of pre-mortal hell and heavenly inspirations of light, then happiness should also be defined in a way that is different from that prescribed by consumerism. Its advertising agents at present constitute a transition while earlier values such as frugality, family life and altruism are gradually being worn away: 'You

F

ought to give yourself a treat!' Among those addressed by advertising, however, are fewer and fewer anal collectors and silent epicures. The genital conqueror has become a chief model and happiness is not to be found in collecting and consuming, but in taking possession of and occupying something that had previously been possessed and occupied by others. The central concern of advertising is no longer the object to be purchased, but the event of purchasing itself, which is seen as pleasurable. The principal aspect, with the help of which the religious tradition tried to define happiness, is becoming less and less intelligible as an experience of grace.

The young man and woman on the television screen, to whom no element of religion still clings, are quite without grace. They have no need of grace, nor do they expect to receive it. It occurs to no one to say 'May God give you his grace' to them when he sees them, though this was the promise, the hope and the desire that emerged in our civilisation when this couple appeared. An aura of fragile happiness surrounded the young people and made them, as we were still able to say in our language, 'touching'. What is more, we can no longer even wish this modern TV model 'good luck'. What is the purpose of that? They can always buy what they want and fulfil their expectations! Our very wish freezes on our lips and an icy cold pattern of relationships that have been set free from all longings radiates from our television screens into every living room.

Grace is a concept that defines the depths of our possible happiness. When I, in what Jaspers would have called my unconditional existential state, choose life, when integration and decision come together and when I have given my full consent and have entered fully into the battle against cynicism, I experience something that is at the basis of all real happiness, at least in so far as it can be expressed in language within the framework of our traditional culture. I am also conscious of the fact that my entry into this state, in which certain parts of my own wishes are for the first time set free, is not the result of my own achievement. I do not have my consent at my disposal. I am not the boss and I forget that I wanted to be in control. 'Not having at one's disposal' is the other category that is used in existential philosophy and that cannot be forgotten without great loss. Every time we give our consent, we are responding and this responsive character is part of the experience of happiness. Happiness is not simply speaking to someone in his situation—it is also responding and corresponding to him. It is a process of integration into the game of taking and giving, not simply taking, getting, appropriating for oneself or simply acting, making or giving. It is grace and the more grace is experienced in happiness, the deeper the happiness is.

A young reader who is untouched by the religious tradition may perhaps wonder how I know this. I would reply to him in this way: The frontiers of my language are the frontiers of my world. The wealth of my language is the wealth that I can experience. The tradition in which I am placed has provided me with a language which interprets my experience, clarifies it, makes it translucent and enriches it. One of the important words in that language is grace. That word provides me with a concept of happiness that has always seemed to me to be more attractive than anything else that I have been offered. In that concept, I found that my ability to desire was respected, my fears were handled carefully and my need for meaning was taken very seriously. My capacity for happiness grew as my linguistic ability increased (and, indeed, as my capacity for suffering also increased; that could be found in my traditional language under the key-word 'repentance').

It is for this reason that I find consumerism and the whole apparatus of existence that has produced it to be an attack against my human dignity. It is also why I do not regard the term 'national massacre', which Pasolini used in this context, in an attempt to describe what happens every day in consumer societies, as at all exaggerated. The use of such a term at least presupposes an emphatic understanding of life of the kind outlined in this article, in other words, a framework of heaven and hell. The unconditional existential aspect is left lying on the way between the technocratic apparatus and consumerism. The structural repression of the existential element makes young people today feel that they are being suffocated. A conservative attitude is seen to be the simplest solution, but it is just as impotent as Jaspers' attitude in 1931, when confronted with Hitler and fascism in Germany.

It should be possible to rediscover religion as a language to be used against the secular trivialisation of man reduced to a function, speech without expressiveness and relationships that have been set free from all longings. What reason could there be for exchanging a life led between heaven and hell for such a secularised and trivialised life? Why should we abandon a tradition that is concerned with bread and wine, fear and guilt, coitus and birth and death and the kingdom of God as unsaleable parts of life? It is, after all, a tradition which has again and again transcended what can be said in the terminology of the social sciences in favour of a promise of life for all men. It is also a tradition in which it has always been possible for one man to claim the unseen light for others: 'May God make his face to shine upon us' (Ps. 67:1).

Translated by David Smith

Notes

1. For what follows, see Dorothee Sölle 'Du sollst keine andern Jeans haben neben mir' *Stichworte zur Geistigen Situation der Zeit* ed. J. Habermas (Frankfurt 1979).

2. K. Jaspers *Die geistige Situation der Zeit* (1931).

3. Pier Paolo Pasolini *Freibeuterschriften. Die Zerstörung der Kultur des Einzelnen durch die Konsumgesellschaft* (Berlin 1978).

Michael Fahey

Joseph Ratzinger as Ecclesiologist and Pastor

LONG BEFORE Joseph Ratzinger was appointed by Paul VI as Archbishop of Munich and Freising he had had a distinguished ministry as priest and theologian in the Catholic Church. Expert at Vatican II, active member of the papal International Theological Commission under the auspices of the Congregation for the Doctrine of the Faith, he received much attention. Although his writings have not been as widely read internationally as some other German theologians, still several of his works have been popular and scholars have appreciated his historical and systematic works concerning the episcopacy, ministry, the Eucharist, eschatology and other issues. Since the accession of Pope John Paul II, Ratzinger has been an appreciated advisor; with Cardinal Höffner he urged the German Episcopal Conference to ask the Vatican to take action against Hans Küng to remove his 'canonical mission' for teaching official Catholic doctrine. Thus, to understand what is transpiring in today's Catholic Church it is important to understand Ratzinger's own assessment of Church life and theology since Vatican II. To date only occasional publications have studied Ratzinger's theological method and perspectives.[1] One is led then to read from an impressive list of his publications to form an overall synthesis of his ecclesiology. His thought shows an amazing consistency. The emergence of cautious warnings in recent years is not based on some new dramatic conversion but is the logical conclusion of years of reflection. Prior to Vatican II he expressed impatience with the lack of vitality in Catholic theology and wrote critically about procedures in the Roman Curia. Shortly after the Council he grew more and more convinced that its real goals had been misunderstood or distorted by certain theologians.

1. THE SETTING IN UNIVERSITY AND CHURCH

Joseph Ratzinger was born in Marktl-an-Inn in Southern Bavaria on 16 April 1927. One of three children born to a police commissioner and his wife, he felt called at an early age to the priesthood. However, at the age of sixteen he was required to enter the German army. After a brief period of military service including posting along the Hungarian border, he was captured by the Americans and held prisoner for some six months until the end of the war. Then in 1946 he entered a seminary, the

Philosophisch-Theologische Hochschule in Freising and shortly afterwards began studies in theology at the University of Munich under professors such as Romano Guardini and Gottlieb Söhngen. Ordained in 1951 to the priesthood, he served as an assistant parish priest in Munich while continuing to study at the University. He obtained the DrTheol in 1953 for research done on the ecclesiology of St Augustine, published as *Volk und Haus Gottes in Augustins Lehre von der Kirche* (Munich 1954). Still continuing his pastoral work he did further studies toward the *Habilitation* (a post-doctoral degree required for teaching in German universities). This time his research was centred not on the fifth century but on the thirteenth-century mystical theologian St Bonaventure, leading to the publication of *Die Geschichtstheologie des heiligen Bonaventura* (Munich 1959).

In the following years Ratzinger moved frequently before returning to Munich. First in 1958 he taught at Freising, then from 1959 to 1963 at Bonn. In 1963 he accepted a position at the University of Münster. From 1966 to 1969 he was professor at the Catholic Theological Faculty of the University of Tübingen where his colleagues included Hans Küng. With Küng he inaugurated a new series of books on dogmatic theology. Soon the atmosphere in Tübingen struck Ratzinger as somewhat tense and inhospitable. Thus when the University of Regensburg offered him a position in its recently established Faculty of Catholic Theology he readily accepted. There also his brother, a priest, was director of a famed boys choir. Until 1977, when he was appointed Archbishop of Munich and successor to Julius Cardinal Döpfner, he taught at Regensburg.

During this period from 1962-65 he had participated at Vatican II as a young theologian, first as personal advisor to Cardinal Frings and later as an official *peritus*. Following this came the appointment as one of some forty theologians to the Vatican International Theological Commission. He influenced several of its important documents especially one on theological pluralism.[2] In 1972 because of a growing uneasiness with critical theology he withdrew his support from the journal *Concilium* and founded with Hans Urs von Balthasar a conservative theological review *Internationale Katholische Zeitschrift/Communio*.

2. EARLY YEARS AS THEOLOGIAN

As early as 1960 while in Bonn, Ratzinger composed an important essay entitled 'Theologia perennis?' which included remarks about his uneasiness concerning contemporary Catholic thought, one so highly westernised, European in character that it appeared to people of other cultures as a foreign import. Too much of theology, he wrote, had become confined, extremely complicated, petrified, because of stultifying philosophical and cultural systems devoid of vitality. He hoped that the coming council would waken the dogmas of faith out of their systematised paralysis without removing what is truly valid.[3]

Shortly afterwards in 1962 he published a study about the New Testament concept of *parrēsia* (free expression, boldness), a virtue extolled in Acts 2:29, 4:13, etc. He considered the delicate question of how one was to conduct oneself with the weak and sinful Church. He spoke of the need for boldness and prophetic utterance. 'The servility of the sycophants (branded by the genuine prophets of the Old Testament as "false prophets"), of those who shy from and shun every collision, who prize above all their calm complacency, is not true obedience. . . . What the Church needs today as always, are not adulators to extol the *status quo*, but men whose humility and obedience are not less than their passion for truth: men who face every misunderstanding and attack as they bear witness; men who, in a word, love the Church more than ease and the unruffled course of their personal destiny.'[4] He was particularly critical of the Catholic Church for 'holding the reins a bit too tightly, for the creation of too many norms, so that not a few of these norms helped abandon the century to disbelief rather than save it'. He also criticised the Church for 'entrenching herself behind exterior safeguards instead of relying on the truth, which is inherent in liberty and shuns such defences'.

This call for openness was repeated in a lecture first given at Tübingen, this time in regard to the Vatican's reactions to the *Dutch Catechism*. Although not happy with some of the Catechism's treatments (its Christology, its doctrine of redemption, its Eucharistic doctrine), still Ratzinger praised its real strengths that sprung from deep, religious feeling. He defended Rome's right to react and to express reservations about the Catechism but noted: 'At the same time we must deplore the fact that Rome inspired such strict secrecy on the Cardinals' Commission and the Commission of Theologians, thereby preventing not only the spread of reliable information but also the furtherance of constructive debate.'[5]

Linked with these critical comments was Ratzinger's typical concern which has remained constant in his pastoral ministry, namely the commitment to protect the simple believers. Once he wrote how struck he had been in 1959 when he stumbled upon a passage in *Compendium of World Religions* by the ex-Catholic Friederich Heiler who begrudgingly admitted that, despite the ambiguities of the Catholic Church, still many millions of people had considered the Roman Church as spiritual mother. After recalling that remark, Ratzinger added in the epilogue to his commentary on Vatican II: 'In the final analysis the Church lives, in sad as well as joyous times, from the faith of those who are simple of heart. This is the way that Israel lived even in the times when Pharasaic legalism and Sadducean liberalism defaced the countenance of the chosen people.'[6]

This comment about the simple believer helps one to comprehend his attitudes towards theology and the Church's pastoral mission. Twenty years later, in a sermon given on 31 December 1979, following the outcry caused by the silencing of Hans Küng, he stated: 'The Christian believer is a simple person: bishops should protect the faith of these little people against the power of intellectuals.'[7]

3. WORRIES ABOUT A COUNCIL MISUNDERSTOOD

At the German Katholikentag, held at Bamberg in 1966, Joseph Ratzinger delivered an analysis of what he saw to be the effects of Vatican II. This speech should be required reading for all wishing to understand his present assessment of Church life. Now begins a gloominess and depression about undesirable developments in the wake of the council. 'Let me start off by admitting quite frankly that there prevails amongst us today a certain air of dissatisfaction, an atmosphere of depression and even of disappointment, such as often follows on festive moments of great joy and exaltation.'[8] In this address he supported of course liturgical reform, the Church's greater openness to the world, and efforts toward Church unity. But the overall assessment is quite grim. In the liturgy he found faulty fascination with the archaic as well as excessive modernisation; the Church's relationship with the world has led it to carelessly turn away from the Cross; finally, in the name of Church unity, some are succumbing to a naïve impetuosity (*Voreiligkeit*) hoping to eliminate controversial theology.

Some of this mood is reflected too in his Tübingen lectures given in 1967, later published as his most widely read work *Introduction to Christianity*. Here he fears that theology has watered down the demands of faith and led to impoverishment. Certain unnamed theologians have been minimising Christian belief. In their struggle with the Church these theologians 'can no longer see in it anything but the human struggle for power, the petty struggle of those who, with their claim to administer official Christianity seemed to stand most in the way of the true spirit of Christianity'.[9] And yet he notes 'the Church is most present not where organising, reforming and governing are going on but in those who simply believe and receive from her the gift of faith that is life to them'.

It would be an instructive exercise to compare the methods of pastoral theology implicit in Ratzinger's *Introduction to Christianity* with Küng's *On Being a Christian*, especially to note the different audiences for which the books are intended. Ratzinger writes largely for the believer, for those close to the Church, some of whom are bothered with changes, some of whom might be unfortunately even driven to the arms of Archbishop Lefebvre, the integralists. Küng on the other hand is writing for the distant, those who are alienated from the Church, those for whom Church can be a stumbling block, who see certain inconsistencies in Church life as a lack of orthopraxis. Were Ratzinger not a university professor himself one might falsely detect a hint of anti-intellectualism in his sentiments. This is not the case. It is rather a distinctly spiritualist, eschatological emphasis to his writings.

In a radio talk given on Christmas 1969 Ratzinger speculated about the Church in the year 2000. His concerns were not about structural changes or reforms but about the intensity of faith. His forecast was that by the century's end unrest will have subsided, a smaller Church will prevail. 'In faith and prayer it will again recognise its true centre and experience the sacraments again as the worship of God and not as a subject for liturgical scholarship.'[10]

About this time Ratzinger collaborated with Hans Urs von Balthasar in a gloomy assessment of the Catholic Church's situation. In a style uncharacteristically marked by overstatement and exaggeration he explained 'Why I Am Still in the Church'. The Church, he wrote, had entered a Babylonian captivity. 'In the midst of a world striving for unity the Church is falling apart in nationalistic partisanship, in calumniation of the alien and glorification of self.'[11] He wondered out loud whether there could be no middle way between the iconoclasts and those who clung to externals from the past, some middle ground between what he called contempt for tradition and mechanical dependence. Again he worried about the simple faithful who have no voice. They are the ones who exercise the true mission of the Church: prayer, bearing daily life with patience, always listening to the word of God. Meanwhile in his view intensive efforts to reform the Church have caused everything else to be forgotten. Reform has been dissociated from the hard work of repentance and concentrated on matters of only secondary importance.

About this time Ratzinger began to object to political theology and the various perspectives of theologies of liberation. He warned against those who have borrowed too much from philosophers ranging from Marx to Marcuse and who have created the impression that we can have a sorrow-free world through social reform alone. He does not name any theologian or group specifically. But in 1972 he laid the blame for confusion and conflict caused by those who fostered 'a new mentality which is based on increasingly "sociologising" of the question of truth'. He reminded the hierarchy of its special function 'of keeping open the question of truth, or insisting on its acceptance, as opposed to the retreat into positivism and sociology'.[12] He later criticised the emphasis on orthopraxis that had marked the fourth world assembly of the World Council of Churches in Uppsala in 1968. According to his understanding of that perspective 'truth is considered as unattainable and its proclamation only an alibi for group interests which are thus consolidated. Only praxis can decide the value or lack of value of theories.'[13] Given that judgment, his opposition is understandable.

In 1972, in association with Hans Urs von Balthasar, Karl Lehmann, Henry de Lubac and others, Ratzinger launched a new journal the *Internationale Katholische*

Zeitschrift/Communio. This publication edited in several languages was intended as a counter-weight to *Concilium*. In its very first page, a colleague, Franz Greiner, set the stage. What the Church has inherited in the post-Vatican II age is abundant but often confusing wares (*reiche, oft verwirrende Angebot*). 'We are increasingly conscious in the Church community that fronts are forming, that a polarisation is taking place, not only of opinions but of views and attitudes that involve the faith and endanger the common basis of belief on which we all stand. We are not prepared to accept this development as an inevitable process.'[14] This journal has become the principal vehicle for Ratzinger's publications even to this date.

Following the publication of *Mysterium Ecclesiae*, the instruction of the Congregation for the Doctrine of the Faith, on 24 June 1973, condemning erroneous doctrines related to the theology of the Church, Ratzinger agreed that the Church had entered a stage of difficult inner tensions and ferment. 'It is now quite clear that organs directing the Church in this situation cannot simply remain silent, but must do their duty in order to master the crisis. The call for clear guidelines is heard ever more acutely and yet, up to now, pope and bishops have been unable to reach a decision.'[15]

By 1975 he tended to blame much of the unrest in the Church on erroneous interpretations of the Pastoral Constitution on the Church in the Modern World, *Gaudium et spes*. According to Ratzinger, some theologians handpicked favourite passages from the Constitution, tacked on selected passages from the Declaration on Religious Freedom, appealed to the Council's openness to world religions, and then on the basis of these texts would tolerate no stand-still (*Stehenbleiben*). 'What devastated (*verwüstete*) the Church of the last decade was not the Council but the refusal to accept it in its totality.'[16]

4. SERVICE IN THE CHURCH TODAY

Today Joseph Ratzinger devotes much of his energies as theologian to clarifying and defending decisions taken by the pope and Roman Curia for the re-establishment of solidarity and authority. His perception of theology's mission seems to come close to that ideal expressed by Pope Pius XII in *Humani Generis* (1950) which stated about theologians: 'It is their duty to indicate how what is taught by the living magisterium is found, either implicitly or explicitly, in Scripture and in divine tradition' (DS 3886). His views about the responsibilities of theologians are similar to those implied in the recent Constitution *Sepientia christiana*, issued 15 April 1979, by the Congregation for Catholic Education concerning ecclesiastical universities. According to the Constitution theology should serve the ministry of unity that rests with bishops and pope. Theology is therefore closely allied to proclamation, catechesis, evangelisation, and should be done under the close supervision of the hierarchical magisterium whence comes the theologian's 'canonical mission' to teach Catholic theology.

One example of this was Ratzinger's defence of the decree by the Congregation for the Doctrine of the Faith concerning the exclusion of women from the priesthood, *Inter Insigniores*, a document which was made public on 27 January 1977 and which occasioned serious controversy. His theological evaluation entitled 'The Male Priesthood: A Violation of Women's Rights?' stated that the conflict that ensued in the Church was a conflict between a functionalist conception of law and a sacramental conception of Church. The sacramental view recognises 'pre-existing symbolic structures of creation, which contain an immutable testimony'. The priesthood is not a career at the disposal of the institutional Church but is an independent, pre-existing datum.[17]

Cardinal Ratzinger also published a pastoral letter in support of the Vatican directive requiring children to make their first confession before their first communion. In this letter he drew upon his own research in Eucharistic theology, liturgy and Church life.[18]

In a sermon given at festivities to celebrate the tenth anniversary of the founding of the Catholic Theology Faculty at Regensburg, Ratzinger returned to a familiar theme, the unchangeable and changeable in the Church. He reiterated his unhappiness about the force of liberation theologies in the Catholic community world-wide, reminding his congregation that it is not by bread alone that man lives.[19]

After publication of Hans Küng's *On Being a Christian* Ratzinger intensified his public criticism of Küng's theology both in regard to infallibility and Christology. Earlier he had joined with other theologians to criticise *Infallible?*.[20] He admitted that he felt pained after years of untroubled collaboration with Küng at Tübingen to have to protest at his former colleague's conclusions. But he objected to Küng's militant vocabulary which seemed to exhibit a lack of respect for the Church. He found some of his historical arguments weak; he objected to Küng's tendentious separation of the terms 'Roman' and 'Catholic'. He reasoned that Küng was attacking not just a theological school of thought, but was denying a fundamental tenet of Catholicism. This conviction remained with him until 1979 when he urged the removal of Küng's *missio canonica*. Ratzinger also published two severe critiques of *On Being a Christian*. At one point it becomes clear that he is suspicious of Küng's pastoral experience for he writes in sharp language: 'If, in drawing up his theology, Küng had been rather more in touch with Church life, he would have been aware that the real anchor-point of the doctrine of the Trinity is Baptism.'[21]

Ratzinger had also entered into some conflicts with Karl Rahner. Although he had joined with Rahner to oppose Küng's view of infallibility, Ratzinger and his colleague Hans Meier published a work on the limits and dangers of democracy in the Church.[22] Here he criticised Rahner's views developed in *Freiheit und Manipulation in Gesellschaft und Kirche* (1970) about the usefulness and legitimacy of establishing a national synod composed of bishops, priests and laity. He found this idea of a mixed synod as a permanent form of higher authority in the Church a total chimera. He likewise found it inconceivable that a lay person could ever exercise authority over a diocese.

The Cardinal again came into conflict with Karl Rahner in a tense affair connected with the University of Munich. When it came time to replace the retiring professor of theology Heinrich Fries in 1979, an appointments committee of the Faculty of Catholic Theology submitted a list of three candidates arranged in order of preference. This was submitted, as is required, to the Bavarian minister of education Professor Hans Meier who, following the preference of Cardinal Ratzinger, did not appoint the first candidate, Johannes Baptist Metz but the second in line, Heinrich Döring. (Professor Meier later also passed over the first nomination for a chair of liturgical studies in the university, Theodor Maas-Ewerd, and appointed instead Reiner Kaczynski.) Rahner published a strong letter of protest on 16 November 1979, in which he criticised Ratzinger's subtle veto. He claimed that it was precisely Metz's involvement in political theology that Ratzinger opposed. In turn Ratzinger responded publicly in an open letter defending the decision that he felt was based on appropriate pedagogical reasons.[23]

5. CONCLUSION

Can one apply a term such as neo-conservatism to the thought of a theologian of the stature as Joseph Ratzinger? From many points of view the term would seem to be a curious misnomer. Here is a theologian well versed in classical western theology, who

G

has championed collegiality, liturgical reform and is known for his openness to Eastern Orthodoxy. He has always been concerned about the negative impact of the forces of Archbishop Lefebvre. The term neo-conservatism would be valid only if by it one understood this theologian's specific view of pastoral theology, if it implied his conviction that today much of the gospel is being neglected by theologians mesmerised by structural reform in the Church, and if the term implied his emphasis on prayer, worship, self-abnegation. Ratzinger's theology has always been closely related to preaching, indeed one of the volumes of his collected essays was entitled *Dogma und Verkündigung*, dogma and preaching. Ratzinger once remarked that when Abelard transferred the teaching of theology from monastery or church to the lecture hall and a neutral university setting this was a mixed blessing. This made it possible especially in our own day to do theology apart from spiritual practice and to create the impression that it might be taught as any purely academic topic which one might learn as a means of livelihood.[24]

In order to quell much of the unrest that grips the Catholic Church in the beginning of the 1980s, it is crucial that those who pursue a critical theology, or political theology, or the various theologies of liberation, or those striving for Church unity through the achieved consensus emerging from bilateral ecumenical documents, will need to understand the preoccupations of theologian Cardinal Ratzinger whose views seem to correspond so closely with those of the present Bishop of Rome, Pope John Paul II.

Notes

1. For a bibliography of Ratzinger's writings to 1974, see R. Tura 'La teologia di J. Ratzinger' *Studia Patavina* 21 (1974) 145-182. See also his interview with D. O'Grady 'The Ratzinger Round' *Month* 6 (1973) 409-412. An appreciation of his writings appears in A. Fermet *Théologies d'aujourd'hui* (Paris 1973) pp. 93-135.

2. *Die Einheit des Glaubens und der Theologische Pluralismus* (Einsiedeln 1973) esp. pp. 17-51 and 61-67.

3. 'Theologia perennis?' *Wort und Wahrheit* 15 (1960) 179-188. English summary in *Theol. Dig.* 10 (1962) 71-76.

4. 'Free Expression and Obedience in the Church' *The Church: Readings in Theology* (New York 1963) 194-217, here pp. 212, 215.

5. 'The Dutch Catechism: A Theological Appreciation' *Furrow* 22 (1971) 739-754, here p. 739, n. 2.

6. *Theological Highlights of Vatican II* (New York 1966) p. 185.

7. Cited by C. Modehn in *Informations Catholiques Internationales*. 547 (14 February 1980) p. 18.

8. 'Catholicism after the Council' *Furrow* 18 (1967) 3-23, here p. 4.

9. *Introduction to Christianity* (New York 1969) pp. 263, 266.

10. 'What will the Church Look Like in 2000?' *Faith and the Future* (Chicago 1971) 89-106, here p. 105.

11. *Two Say Why* (Chicago 1971) pp. 65-91, here pp. 67, 69.

12. 'What Unites and Divides Denominations?' *Inter. Cath. Rev./Communio* 1 (1972) 115-119, here p. 116.

13. 'Magisterium of the Church, Faith and Morality' *Problems of the Church Today* (Washington 1976) 74-83, here p. 74.

14. *Int. Cath. Rev./Communio* 1 (1972) 1.

15. 'Ökumenisches Dilemma? Zur Diskussion um die Erklärung "Mysterium Ecclesiae"' *Int. Kath. Zeit./Communio* 3 (1974) 56-63, here p. 56.

16. 'Der Weltdienst der Kirche. Auswirkungen von "Gaudium et Spes" in letzten Jahrzehnt' *Int. Kath. Zeit./Communio*.

17. *The Order of Priesthood* (Huntington, Ind. 1978) pp. 127-137, here pp. 131, 134.

18. 'First Confession and First Communion' *Origins* 7 (1978) 558-560.

19. 'Wandelbares und Unwandelbares in der Kirche' *Int. Kath. Zeit./Communio* 7 (1978) 182-184.

20. 'Widersprüche im Buch von Hans Küng' *Zum Problem Unfehlbarkeit* ed. K. Rahner (Freiburg 1971) pp. 97-116.

21. 'On Hans Küng's "Being a Christian"' *Doctrine and Life* 27 (1977) 3-17, here p. 9. For another evaluation of the same book, see 'Wer verantwortet die Aussagen der Theologie?' *Diskussion über H. Küng's Christ-Sein* (Mainz 1976) 7-18.

22. *Demokratie in der Kirche. Möglichkeiten, Grenzen, Gefahren* (Limburg 1970).

23. For an account of Rahner's objections, see *Doctrine and Life* 30 (1980) 34-39.

24. 'Was ist Theologie?' *Int. Kath. Zeit./Communio* 8 (1979) 121-128.

Jeffrey Kay

Hans Urs von Balthasar, a Post-critical Theologian?

AT THE 1979 National Convention of the American Academy of Religion in New York City there was a meeting of the 'Seminar on Dialectics' devoted to the discussion of Robert Doran's *Subject and Psyche: Ricoeur, Jung and the Search for Foundations*.[1] The series of annual seminars was begun by students of Lonergan, and Doran himself is powerfully influenced by Lonergan. During the course of the seminar Doran argued that he had in this book done the foundation work for a new systematic poetic theology. The only theologian he could think of who had already begun work on such a theology was Hans Urs von Balthasar. This surprising, close association of Balthasar with people like Jung, Ricoeur and Lonergan is alluded to by Leo O'Donovan when he writes: 'In fact, through his own special attention to symbolism and aesthetics I think Balthasar stands in many ways closer to current forms of critical theology than is generally recognised.'[2]

The shift that is taking place in contemporary religious and theological thinking has been accompanied by a broad sociological phenomenon that has been analysed frequently.[3] The movement has received thoughtful expression through the journal *Parabola, Myth and the Quest for Meaning* now in its fifth volume and published by the Society for the Study of Myth and Tradition in New York City. An important manifestation of the shift within Catholic theology is the emphasis placed by Bernard Lonergan on feeling and on symbolic language as the language of feeling in his *Method in Theology*,[4] in stark contrast to the emphasis on the intellectual in *Insight*.[5]

1. RICOEUR AND BALTHASAR

An important impetus towards this shift was given by Paul Ricoeur in his conclusion to *The Symbolism of Evil*,[6] entitled 'The Symbol Gives Rise to Thought'. He writes there of our contemporary situation as follows: 'The historical moment of the philosophy of symbols is that of forgetfulness and restoration. Forgetfulness of hierophanies, forgetfulness of the signs of the sacred, loss of man himself in so far as he belongs to the sacred. The forgetfulness, we know, is the counterpart of the great task of nourishing men, of satisfying their needs by mastering nature through a planetary technique. It is in the age when our language has become precise, more univocal, more technical in a word, more suited to those integral formalisations which are called precisely symbolic logic, it is in this very age of discourse that we want to recharge our language, that we want to start again from the fullness of language.' 'Beyond the desert of criticism, we wish to be called again.'[7] Criticism has laid the foundation for this restoration by demythologising sacred texts, i.e., by distinguishing the historical and pseudo-historical; by dissolving myth as explanation it has made room for myth as symbol.[8] It has opened the way to a second naïvete, a mediated immediacy which is the post-critical equivalent of the precritical hierophany. This conjunction of belief and criticism demythologises but does not demythicise. Although Ricoeur refers to Jung as one of the demythologisers, he would probably change 'demythologise' to 'demythicise' in the following statement of Jung's and then endorse it. 'How, then, can one possibly "demythologise" the figure of Christ? A rationalistic attempt of that sort would soak all the mystery out of his personality, and what remained would no longer be the birth and tragic fate of a God in time, but historically speaking, a badly authenticated religious teacher, a Jewish reformer who was hellenistically interpreted and misunderstood—a kind of Pythagoras, maybe, or, if you like, a Buddha or a Mohammed, but certainly not a Son of God or a God incarnate.'[9] Jung's *Answer to Job* is, I think, an excellent example of what Ricoeur means by second naïvete and has a profound affinity with the naïve, childlike, seemingly literal way in which Balthasar deals with biblical texts.

A good way to formulate what Balthasar finds lacking in Bultmann and in many contemporary 'liberal' theologians is their inability to distinguish demythologising and demythicising. They are unable to pass beyond the desert of criticism to this second naïvete. They continually want to interpret the Christian myth by explaining it conceptually in such a way that it is no longer clear that the confessing Christian has anything significant that the 'anonymous Christian' lacks. Many 'liberals' tend unintentionally towards what Ricoeur and Balthasar call reductive interpretations that clear away the symbolic base. 'These interpretations are readily expressed as follows: such and such a symbol seemed to intend to say something new in regard to a referential field that was only intimated or anticipated; finally, after due consideration, the symbol signifies only this positing of desire, that class membership, such a degree of strength or weakness of fundamental will. In relation to this true discourse, symbolic discourse becomes synonymous with illusory discourse.'[10] As Balthasar points out, Rahner is ready to say that certain Christological statements in the New Testament were not misleading then but have become misleading now.[11] Liberal theologians are losing their sensitivity to precisely what Ricoeur calls the 'something new' intended by the symbol. Such reductive interpretations are consistent, Ricoeur claims, with the semantic aim characteristic of the speculative order. 'Every interpretation aims at relocating the semantic outline sketched by metaphorical utterance inside an available horizon of understanding that can be mastered conceptually.' This leads, however, to a 'destruction of the metaphorical by the conceptual'. Ricoeur calls, therefore, for a mode of interpretation that is both metaphorical and conceptual. 'On the one side, interpretation seeks the clarity of the concept; on the other, it hopes to preserve the dynamism of meaning that the concept holds and pins down.' 'Metaphor is living by virtue of the fact that it introduces the spark of imagination into a "thinking more" at the conceptual level. This struggle to "think more", guided by the "vivifying principle", is the "soul" of interpretation.'[12] If Balthasar is weak on the conceptual side of interpretation (he admits that Rahner is much the greater speculative thinker),[13] he relentlessly reminds the liberals of the centrality of the metaphorical side, at which he excels.

Balthasar can be seen to compensate liberals similarly when Ricoeur speaks of the polarity in interpretation as a hermeneutical circle consisting of believing in order to understand and understanding in order to believe.[14] Balthasar, a lover of Anselm, excels at the former whereas the liberals excel at the latter. Post-critical hermeneutics, 'must make its presuppositions explicit, state them as beliefs, and try to make the wager pay off in understanding. Such a wager is the contrary of an apologetics that pretends to lead reflection, without a break, from knowledge towards belief. A philosophy that begins with symbols proceeds in the opposite direction, in accordance with an essentially Anselmian schema.'[15]

The epochal significance of this post-critical interpretation appears perhaps most clearly in the following statement by Ricoeur: 'Consequently the task of the philosopher guided by symbols would be to break out of the enchanted enclosure of consciousness of oneself, to end the prerogative of self-reflection. The symbol gives reason to think that the *Cogito* is within being, and not *vice versa*. Thus second naïvete would be a second Copernican revolution.'[16] It is into this 'enchanted enclosure' that Balthasar understands Rahner to be inviting us when he calls on us to move more quickly towards the 'reception of the Enlightenment into the contemporary Church'.[17] Possibly Balthasar's sensitivity to symbols will help to draw contemporary theology away from the temptation to settle down in Enlightenment hermeneutics at just the time when non-theological thought is making a second Copernican revolution into a post-critical hermeneutics.[18]

2. JUNG AND BALTHASAR

In addition to Ricoeur, Doran also indicated an affinity between Balthasar and Jung. In 1956 Balthasar wrote: 'Hence we have no objection in principle to investigating the phenomenology of the natural religions in the light of a total philosophical anthropology; if Jung's research is really this, if it does not deny all genuine transcendence by reducing it to purely psychological categories, it can be considered fruitful and necessary.'[19] In 1961 he attacked Jung for having 'dissolved and denigrated the images of God to psychic archetypes that one can "take care of" "therapeutically" because they are nothing more than compositions of the collective unconscious'.[20] In 1974 in the title essay in *Pneuma und Institution*[21] he makes a significant positive reference to Jung. He refers to Jung's concepts of 'anima' and 'animus' to support his argument that males must integrate their femininity and females their masculinity. Although there are severe criticisms that must be made of the limitations of Jung's notion of the anima,[22] there can be no doubt that it lies at the very heart of his psychology. He is speaking primarily to adult western males whom he describes as predominantly extraverted,[23] and therefore soulless. One of his publications was entitled *Modern Man in Search of a Soul* and this well summarises his major concern. The soul for him was feminine and the male is dependent on the female to help him find his soul, or his femininity. Of woman he writes: 'Woman, with her very dissimilar psychology, is and always has been a source of information about things for which a man has no eyes. She can be his inspiration; her intuitive capacity, often superior to man's, can give him timely warning, and her feeling, always directed towards the personal, can show him ways which his own less personally accented feeling would never have discovered.'[24] Although it is highly debatable how accurately that statement can be said of all women, it is certainly an accurate description of what western culture has most admired when it spoke of 'the feminine'. The anima is that aspect of the feminine that leads a male ego to individuation by mediating between it and the collective unconscious.[25] According to Erich Neumann the anima is 'the vehicle *par excellence* of the transformative character [of the feminine]. It is the mover, the instigator of change, whose fascination drives, lures, and encourages the male to all the adventures of the soul and spirit, of action and creation in the inner and the outward world.'[26] She 'confronts the ego hero with a "trial" that he must withstand . . . it compels tension, change and an intensification of the personality'.[27] 'It is the closest to consciousness and to the ego of all the forms that the feminine can assume in the male psyche.'[28]

There is an obvious affinity between Jung's concern with the role of the anima and Balthasar's central concern for the role of Mary, whom Jung discusses frequently as an image of the anima. Mary is the spotless soul of the Church whose active readiness and receptivity allowed Christ to reveal himself completely. As the living realisation of total Christian faith, which is a fundamentally feminine act, Mary is the model for all Christians. In addition to his books on Thérèse of Lisieux and Elizabeth of Dijon, another powerful source of his insight into the femininity, i.e., in its anima character, of Christian faith is Adrienne von Speyr about whom he has written: 'In Basel, the mission of Adrienne von Speyr (which, in view of her books, can no longer remain incomprehensible to a Christian public) was decisive. What Ignatius intended in his time henceforth meant for me 'secular institute'; the hard sacrifice [he refers to leaving the Jesuits] which the transition demanded was accompanied by the certainty of serving the same idea more exactly. It was Adrienne von Speyr who showed the way in which Ignatius is fulfilled by John, and therewith laid the basis for most of what I have published since 1940. Her work and mine are neither psychologically nor philologically to be separated; two halves of a single whole, which has as its centre a single foundation.'[29] Such a statement, coupled with their co-founding of a secular institute for women, his publication of thirty-one books by her and one book about her, and his writing a book about her, all point to how important she was in his relationship to the anima and how important he feels she is for the modern Church in its relation to the anima.[30] He frequently speaks of Mary as the *anima ecclesiastica* and of the Christian being transformed into an *anima ecclesiastica*, a churched soul.

How important the anima aspect of the feminine is for Balthasar appears clearly in the essays 'Pneuma und Institution' and 'Kenose der Kirche?'[31] The essays also illustrate his second naïvete, his skill as a post-critical interpreter, a skill that Jung had and a skill that demands the integration of a more feminine intuition and belief with a more masculine critical and speculative ability.

The essay, 'Pneuma und Insitution', begins by discussing interpersonal human relations and particularly the marital relation in order to shed light on the Trinity and then on the relation between the Spirit and the Church as institution.[32] He calls this approach naïf and simple. The interpersonal relationship demands of each partner a unified disposition of emptiness and fullness, of activity and passivity, of being actively in pursuit of the best possible passivity. This is best described in erotic categories, whereby the primary experience is a feminine one of being broken through and shaped in order then to express itself and shape others in a masculine way. Each partner must be both masculine and feminine and it is not important which takes the initiative. The fruit of the erotic union will always be the unexpected, the unhoped-for and may be the mysterious and unhoped-for gift of a new personal being. This relation is analogous to the reciprocal, masculine-feminine relationship between the Father and Son bearing fruit in the Holy Spirit. The outpouring of the Spirit parallels Christ giving his body and blood to his bride, the Church.[33] Christ and Mary each encompass in themselves both masculinity and femininity. That the masculine/feminine relation is both heavenly and earthly is expressed in a startling way when Balthasar draws on the image of Sophia as the heavenly Jerusalem. He applies the Genesis/Ephesians statement about a man leaving his mother and father to cling to his wife, to the Son leaving the Father and the heavenly Jerusalem to cling to his bride, the Church.[34]

It is in order to preserve the symbol of the sexual polarity within the Trinity and between Christ and the Church that Balthasar argues against women priests. Because Peter and the twelve on the one hand and Mary on the other have two different roles in the Church and because Mary's is the larger, more embracing one, women would be abandoning a more significant for a less significant symbolic function if they were to become priests. Such a move would only contribute to our modern culture's neglect of the feminine.[35] One could readily suspect this as a rationalisation for excluding women from positions of power within the Church. An indication, however, of how important Balthasar does think women are in the Church might be found in an article by A. Peelman which justifies women priests on the basis of Balthasar's writings.[36] Perhaps his opposition to women priests is based on his failure consistently to distinguish masculine and male, feminine and female as he has done earlier. Although he is emphatic about males representing the feminine in the Trinity, Christ and Mary, he is reluctant to see women representing the masculine in those realities. His fundamental reason seems to be less the maleness of Christ and the twelve disciples and more his awareness of the need to have the feminine in its anima aspect clearly represented in our overly-masculine culture.

This awareness is at the heart of his criticism of liberal theologians.[37] As Jung clearly indicates, the tendency to stay in a critical hermeneutics and not move to a post-critical one, i.e., the tendency to explain symbols away, is rooted in the failure of modern culture to appropriate the anima character of the feminine. Rather than conservative, Balthasar ought more properly to be called compensatory and perhaps even prophetic.

Notes

1. Washington 1979.
2. 'God's Glory in Time' *Communio* 2 (1975) 268.
3. Jacob Needleman *New Religions* (Garden City 1970); Robert Wuthnow *Experimentation in American Religion: the New Mysticisms and their Implications for the Churches* (Berkeley 1978); Robert Ellwood *Alternative Altars, Unconventional and Eastern Spirituality in America* (Chicago 1979).
4. London and New York 1972.
5. London and New York 1967.
6. New York 1967.
7. Ricoeur, *ibid.* 349.
8. *Ibid.* 350.
9. *Answer to Job* Par. 647 in *The Collective Works of C. G. Jung* (Princeton 1969).
10. Ricoeur *The Rule of Metaphor* (Toronto 1977) p. 302.
11. *Neue Klarstellungen* (Einsiedeln 1979) p. 47.
12. Ricouer *The Rule of Metaphor* p. 303.
13. *Herder Korrespondenz* 30 (1976) 75.
14. Ricoeur *Symbolism of Evil* p. 353.
15. *Ibid.* p. 357.
16. *Ibid.* p. 356.
17. *Neue Klarstellungen* p. 44f.
18. On postmodern epistemology, see Gregory Bateson *Mind and Nature: A Necessary Unity* (New York 1980).
19. *The God Question and Modern Man* (New York 1967) p. 77.
20. *Herrlichkeit, I, Schau der Gestalt* (Einsiedeln 1961) p. 480.
21. Einsiedeln (1974) p. 209.
22. See James Hillman 'Anima I and II' in *Spring* (1973-74).
23. 'The Relations between the Ego and the Unconscious' in *Collected Works of C. G. Jung* VII (Princeton 1966) Par. 303.

24. *Ibid.*, Par. 296.

25. See Ann Belford Ulanov *The Feminine in Jungian Psychology and Christian Theology* (Evanston 1971) p. 232.

26. *The Great Mother* (Princeton 1955) p. 33.

27. *Ibid.* p. 34.

28. *Ibid.* p. 36.

29. *Communio* 2 (1975) 219.

30. Barbara Albrecht *Eine Theologie des Katholischen, Einfuehrung in das Werk Adrienne von Speyr* I (Einsiedeln 1972); Hans Urs von Balthasar *Erster Blick auf Adrienne von Speyr* (Einsiedeln 1968).

31. In 'Pneuma und Institution' pp. 119-132, 201-235.

32. *Ibid.* p. 202.

33. *Ibid.* p. 217.

34. *Ibid.* p. 124.

35. 'Frauenpriestertum?' in *Neue Klarstellungen*, cited in note 11, pp. 109-115.

36. 'Church in the Light of the Christ Event' in *Eglise et theologie* 9 (1978) 169-207.

37. 'Die Spiritualitaet Teilhard de Chardin' in *Word und Wahrheit* 18 (1963) 339-350.

Contributors

GREGORY BAUM was born in Berlin in 1923 but has lived in Canada since 1940, being ordained to the priesthood there in 1954. He studied at McMaster University, Canada, the Ohio State University and at the University of Fribourg and is now professor of theology and sociology at St Michael's College, University of Toronto. He is editor of *The Ecumenist* and assistant editor of the *Journal of Ecumenical Studies*. He has written, amongst other things, *Man Becoming* (1970), *New Horizon* (1972) and *Religion and Alienation* (1975).

MICHAEL A. FAHEY SJ, was born in 1933 and is now professor of ecclesiology and director of graduate studies in the Department of Theological Studies, Concordia University, Montreal, Canada. He had previously studied in Louvain and at the University of Tübingen where he received a DrTheol in 1970. He is author of *Cyprian and the Bible* (Tübingen 1971) and co-author with J. Meyendorff of *Trinitarian Theology East and West* (Brookline, Mass. 1977). He is executive secretary for the Orthodox/Roman Catholic Bilateral Consultation in North America. He has published widely in the area of ecclesiology and ecumenism in *Theological Studies, Concilium, Journal of Ecumenical Studies, Het Christelijk Oosten*, etc. He has recently published several studies of Karl Rahner's ecclesiology.

MICHAEL FLEET is assistant professor of political science, Marquette University, Milwaukee, Wisconsin. He had formerly taught at the Universidad de Chile, Santiago, the University of Southern California, and the Universidad Javeriana and the Universidad de los Andes, Bogota. He has published articles on the Latin American Church, the Latin American automotive industry, and Chilean politics. He is currently working on a study of Chilean Christian Democracy. His publications include *Latin American Institutional Development: The Changing Catholic Church* (Santa Monica 1969).

ED GRACE studied philosophy at the Catholic University of America and theology at the Gregorian University in Rome. He is lecturing professor at Temple University Abroad (Rome, Italy) on religion, culture and social ethics. He is the editor-founder of NTC News—an Italian-based ecumenical news agency specialising in the phenomenon of 'faith-politics'. It is now in its seventh year of publication. He has written various articles on Italian politics, the Vatican and the Dutch Church.

PETER HEBBLETHWAITE was born in Manchester, England, in 1930. He entered the Jesuits in September 1948, and studied philosophy at Chantilly, France, modern languages at Oxford, and theology at Heythrop College. He was assistant editor of *The Month* from 1965, editor from 1967 to 1974. Since leaving the Jesuits on amicable terms, he has worked as a free-lance writer, and from 1976-1979 he has lectured in French literature at Wadham College, Oxford. From September 1979 he has been Vatican affairs correspondent of the *National Catholic Reporter*. His books include *The Runaway Church* (1975, paperback 1977); *Christian-Marxist Dialogue and Beyond* (1977); *The Year of Three Popes* (1978, with Ludwig Kaufman SJ); *John Paul II, Pope for the Year 2000*; *The New Inquisition?* (1980).

EDWARD JOSEPH HOLLAND has been an associate of the Center of Concern since 1973. His primary responsibilities deal with religion and labour linkage, and the world-wide Christian-socialist encounter. Since 1979, he has also been the national co-ordinator of the National Conference on Religion and Labor. He was born in New York City on 18 March 1940, is married, and has two children. Prior to working at the Center of Concern, he did graduate studies and spent 5 years in community work with the Puerto Rican community in the NE, USA and in Puerto Rico. He is a PhD candidate in social ethics from the University of Chicago. He also holds an MA in social ethics from the same University, as well as an MA in religious studies from Niagara University. He did graduate work in social psychology at the New School for Social Research in New York City from 1968-1970, and was a Fulbright Scholar in Chile from 1972-1973. He is author of *The American Journey* (1976) and has published articles in many religious and secular journals and lectures frequently across the United States.

JEFFREY KAY ThD (Basel), is associate professor of religious studies at St Thomas University and author of *Theological Aesthetics, The Role of Aesthetics in the Theological Method of Hans Urs von Balthasar* (Bern/Frankfurt 1975) and 'Aesthetics and a posteriori Evidence in Balthasar's Theological Method' *Communio* 2 (1975) 289-299. He lives with his wife and son in Fredericton, N.B., Canada.

CHRISTOPHER LASCH has taught history in the University of Rochester, USA, since 1970. Among his books are *The New Radicalism in America* (1965); *Haven in a Heartless World: The Family Besieged* (1977); and *The Culture of Narcissism* (1979).

RENÉ LAURENTIN was born in Tours, France, in 1917 and ordained priest in 1946. Having gained a doctorate in letters at the Sorbonne and in theology at the Institut Catholique, Paris, he has since taught theology at the Université de l'Ouest, Angers, as well as been visiting professor at universities in Canada, USA, Italy and Latin America. He was a consultor to the theological preparatory commission for Vatican II and subsequently an expert at the Council itself. He is a member of the Mariological Academy of Rome, vice-president of the Société Française d'Etudes Mariales, a writer for the *Figaro*, and also does pastoral work in Paris. Most of his published works are about the Virgin Mary, Vatican II and synods, and include the following: *Développement et salut, nouveaux ministères et fin du clegé*; *Lourdes. Documents authentiques*; *Visage de Bernadette*; *Jésus et le temple*; *Thérèse de Lisieux, mythe et réalité*; *Pentecôtisme chez les catholiques*.

GEORGES NIVAT was born in Clermont-Ferrand, France, in 1935. After studying in his native city, at the Ecole Normale Supérieure, Paris, at St Anthony's College, Oxford, and in Moscow, he qualified to teach Russian and did so successively in the universities of Toulouse, Lille and Paris, before becoming professor in the University of Geneva, Switzerland. He has written various works on dissidence in Russia and on

Solzhenitsyn in particular, including *Soljenitsyne* (Paris 1980). He has also written many studies of classical Russian writers. He is a member of the editorial board of *Réveil*, the newspaper of the Reformed Church in the region of Rhône-Alpes.

PABLO RICHARD was born in Chile in 1939 and studied philosophy and theology in Austria, Chile, Rome and Paris, where he was awarded a doctorate in sociology in 1978. He is at present lecturer in theology at the National University of Costa Rica, and is a member of the Study Commission for the History of the Church in Latin America (CEHILA). He has published over 30 articles on the theology of liberation and the situation of the Church in Latin America, and five books, including *Le Christianisme à l'épreuve des théologies de la libération* (Lyon 1978) and *Mort des Chrétientés et naissance de l'Eglise* (Paris 1979).

ANDRÉ ROUSSEAU was born in France in 1941 and has a doctorate in sociology from Louvain. He is a lecturer in the sociology of religion and the sociology of knowledge at the Institut Catholique in Paris and director of research at the Centre Lebret. He is the author of *Trois Enquêtes sur les Catholiques* (Lyon 1977) and has contributed to various books on the sociology of religion.

DOROTHEE SÖLLE was born in 1929. She studied theology, philosophy and literature at the universities of Cologne, Freiburg and Göttingen. She graduated at Göttingen and qualified to teach at Cologne. Since 1965, she has taught systematic theology at the Union Theological Seminary, New York. She lives in Hamburg. Her publications include: *Stellvertretung. Ein Kapitel Theologie nach dem 'Tode Gottes'* (Stuttgart 1965); *Atheistisch an Gott glauben* (Olten 1968); *Das Recht, ein anderer zu werden* (Neuwied 1971); *Realisation. Studien zum Verhältnis von Theologie und Dichtung nach der Aufklärung* (Neuwied 1973); *Leiden—Thema der Theologie* (Stuttgart 1973); *Die revolutionäre Geduld. Gedichte* (Berlin 1974); *Die Hinreise. Zur religiöse Erfahrung* (Stuttgart 1974); *Sympathie. Theologisch-politische Traktate* (Stuttgart 1978); *Fliegen lernen. Gedichte* (Berlin 1979); *Wählt das Leben* (Stuttgart 1980).

PETER STEINFELS is executive editor of *Commonweal*, a journal of political, religious, and literary commentary published by Roman Catholic lay people. He attended Loyola University in Chicago and holds a PhD in European history from Columbia University in New York. He has worked in the field of bioethics, editing *The Hastings Center Report*, a journal dealing with ethical issues in science and medicine. He is the co-editor of *Death Inside Out*, a collection of philosophical and historical essays on dying. He has written on political topics for many American journals and is the author of *The Neoconservatives* (New York 1979).

CATHOLIC HERALD

Essential reading for the informed Catholic

- Home news of the Catholic community

- World-wide coverage of religious affairs

- Special Rome correspondent

- Weekly liturgical commentaries

- Comprehensive presentation of controversial issues

- Patrick O'Donovan's Charterhouse column

- John Ryan's cartoons

To avoid disappointment, why not place a regular order with your local newsagent.

Publications from T. & T. Clark

NICENE AND POST-NICENE FATHERS OF THE CHRISTIAN CHURCH: FIRST SERIES

Edited by Philip Schaff

Complete Catalogue free on request

T. & T. CLARK LIMITED
36 George Street
Edinburgh EH2 2LQ
Scotland